I0486711

Zombie Marketing: The Epidemiology of Brand Awareness
© 2015 by Jack Larson

ISBN-13:
978-1517593438

ISBN-10:
1517593433

For all my supporters,
living or undead.

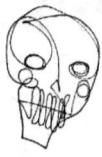

Table of Contents

Introduction: What is Zombie Marketing?

Zombie Marketing is an approach to making your brand as contagious and communicable as a zombie virus. It's a set of strategies and tactics for marketing success built upon The World Health Organization's five main phases of a pandemic. These describe the spread of a virus from patient zero to pandemic status.

Social media marketing works in the same manner, taking obscure brands into international popularity via a mechanism known as Viral Marketing. It has long been understood by advertisers that there is no form of advertising more effective than word of mouth, which also happens to be the most cost-efficient.

Today, with the advent of social media and the ubiquitous smartphone, word of mouth has given way to "electronic word of mouth". Advances in communications technology coupled with the democratization of the means of mass production has made it possible for anyone with a good idea to compete on a level playing field with bigger or more established companies.

Mass marketing, affected by the sudden viability of micro markets, has been augmented by micro marketing, a strategy which targets demographics that are too far outside of the mainstream to be reached by traditional mass marketing tactics. Outside the mainstream, it must be emphasised, does not imply small or unpopular. Prior to the social media revolution of the last decade, niche markets lacked visibility and accessibility Mass appeal, not merit or uniqueness, has traditionally ruled the marketplaces. This has all undergone a change of apocalyptic proportions.

This is an opportune time for all entrepreneurs.The limitations which have traditionally defined relationships between producers and consumers, creators and collectors, writers and readers, musicians and audiences, have been fragmented by the interconnectivity of social media. This reformation of the media landscape has leveled the field of competition, and empowered the independent creator. Creativity and strategic thinking matter more now than a big advertising budget.

This guide explores the use of social media as a tool for exploiting the opportunities which have emerged in the post-apocalyptic context a fragmented marketplace. It is my sincere wish that you find it helpful and applicable to whatever strain of Zombie Virus you're presently formulating in your studio, your basement, or in your own brain.

Jack Larson
9/23/15

Preface

Too many guides are bogged down with minutia, providing detailed click-by-click instructions often accompanied by screen captures, making for an idiot proof set of instructions. This is because they aim at the widest possible audience which, by definition, means the least informed about a given subject.

This is not one of those guides. This is not for "dummies" or "idiots." This was written for creative, productive, entrepreneurial individuals who want to sell their work, whether it is art, music, film, or any other product or service. It was written with the presumption that my readers have already attained some degree of proficiency in their craft and want to turn it into a thriving business.

To make the subject interesting, I replaced standard marketing and sales jargon with metaphors that make the abstractions easier to conceptualize. For example, which of the following makes more sense to you?:

1) "Developing new products and services for existing customers instead of getting new customers for existing products and services to maximize total customer value."

That mess came from The Ultimate Marketing Guide: How to Find Your Most Promotable Edge, Turn it into a Powerful Marketing Message, and Deliver it to the Right Prospects," 2nd edition.

or

2) "Your brand is like a new strain of zombie virus and the key to reaching pandemic status is spreading it into areas where people interact with one another, thus making it easy for them to spread it to their friends."

Obviously, the second sentence is more sensible. The zombie metaphor goes right for the throat. I use it because most of my anecdotal support for the viability of Zombie Marketing comes directly from my own successes and failures as I learned to sell my zombie themed artwork with social media. Because I paint zombies and little else, the art galleries have little place for me outside of Halloween themed shows; however, rather than change my work to fit the limitations imposed by geography and the local marketplace, I learned to use the Internet to overcome those limits and in the process I developed a strategy and a number of tactics which I have since applied to other businesses and have achieved similar results.

Zombie Marketing uses a combination of both standard and unorthodox approaches to building brand awareness. It incorporates social media and a decentralized web presence along with radical pricing strategies to build a sustainable business, and best of all it doesn't require an advertising budget. Do a Google search for "zombie art" right now and take note of my own Internet presence. Out of millions of results, my portfolio usually occupies the first page of search results. Given the fact that I have not paid one cent for advertising, my web presences alone should persuade you to consider applying some of these concepts to your own business model.

Zombie Marketing is a strategy for attaining market saturation. The use of social media as a marketing tool is the same no matter what product, book, service, idea, or brand being promoted. You can adapt these methods to your particular niche and achieve ubiquity without a huge advertising budget thanks to the Web 2.0 revolution. Your workspace is your ground zero, your buyers are the hosts, and your brand is the zombie virus,spreading from initial outbreak to pandemic, striving for market dominance, known here as: World Zombification.

Phase 0: A New Strain is Identified.

The Zombification Process

Your objective is to become a household name, to invade every home with your brand. That may sound too ambitious to contemplate at this stage in your business but it's definitely possible if the proper conditions are established. When you imagine an outbreak of zombieism , do you at any point wonder if they'll stop once they take over a small town? No. Of course not. The horde just gets bigger and moves to the next town, the next city, the next state, the next country, unto the last man on Earth.

How many pop stars do you know about despite your best efforts to remain unaware of their existences? Do you invite every song that gets stuck in your head? Of course not. Effective marketing doesn't give the target an opt-out. Every person, fan or not, is a potential carrier for the Viral Marketing campaign. Therefore, your strategy should incorporate a plan for infecting new markets even if you're working within a relatively small niche.

When a mad scientist engineers his latest strain of Zombie Virus, you can be sure that it's not being designed with constraints in mind. The virus is the chosen catalyst precisely because it has no built in limitations, and nor should your vision about how far your brand can go. This means that you're going to have to ship your work internationally. If you're dealing with digital goods only, you're still going to have to be able to send promotional products anywhere and everywhere, so plan on making mail order a cornerstone of your operation.

Hard copies must accompany digital goods as often as possible. Direct contact is the objective; for your brand to function like a communicable disease, there must be many hosts, each one a potential ground zero for another outbreak. Direct contact leads to more word of mouth activity because the physical product is its own advertisement. Your product must be capable of being a conversation piece. You're marketing to your customers and to those in their social networks, both on and off the Internet.

Your expanding portfolio or catalogue will be the barometer of your success. As long as your work is consistently selling and you're busily producing more of it, you're winning. Even if you barely break even on expenses, you're more than likely improving your work with the constant practice that constant sales entail. Each successful business transaction is itself another guarantee that your brand awareness is expanding. Each sale is a victory and every product delivered serves to remind to the buyer that you're out there. You have to get into their brains.

However, before you can even begin to promote something, you must consider the limitations of the marketplace and your own productive capacity. First turn your creative work into a marketable product. Then you begin optimizing your workflow to accommodate an ever increasing demand. Prepare to sell big long before the big orders arrive. Selling big is not the same thing as "selling out". In today's world, in what some call the New Economy, you can sell big and still maintain total creative control. People who decry "selling out" are usually just people with nothing to offer .There's no shame in entrepreneurialism or in striving to do big things.

This is a long term strategy aimed at creating long term relationships with those who support your brand. Short term successes will occur, however, they require the security of a sustainable business model which makes allowances for risk taking and the inevitable failures which attend risk taking. Your sustainable business model must ride upon the consistent success of one or more products or services which you can reliably sell any day of the week. It can be anything. For me, zombies did the trick. Zombie themed artwork, as it turns out, is an easy product to move. All it took was an efficient production method and access to buyers.

I developed my own production methods while creating a series of paintings entitled "1000 Zombies". I was trying to imagine what my art would look like five-hundred paintings into the future. Then I envisioned what the one thousandth one would look like. I decided to dedicate one thousand paintings to see if my work would show improvement. I knew it could be done if the sale of each painting financed the creation of the next until I arrived at one thousand. As I worked out the logistics of the project, I made the decision to standardize my operating procedures to make progress more trackable and to maintain a constant cash flow throughout the entire one thousand.

The next four chapters demonstrate how I made my brand infectious and ready for dissemination.

Chapter 1: Weaponizing Your Zombie Virus

One of the reasons why zombie viruses have no trouble replicating throughout populations is its ease of transmission. A single exposure is enough to pass it on to the next host. It doesn't require a great deal of time or effort for the infection to be passed along. So too must your product be made transmittable, infectious, and as close to cost-free as possible. This does not imply profit-free; it just means that the money might take an indirect and sometimes circuitous route.

The zombie virus must have a host in which to live and replicate. Outside of a host it cannot function. So too must your product must be liberated from the confines of the workspace and transmitted to the intended audiences. I consider artwork lying around my studio as "dead," as opposed to the work displayed in homes around the world, for in the hands of others, there always remains the possibility that that it might take on new life.

If your ideas remain shelved in a dark corner of the basement there is no chance of anything happening at all. Even a bad plan or rudimentary idea is better than nothing at all. I'm the first to admit that the art I produced early on in my career was rudimentary, and that's putting it nicely. The key here is in recognizing that there is a bond, a symbiotic relationship, between the created thing and its possessor. It is that bond and not money which is the basis of your relationship with your collectors, buyers, fans, or customers. The relationship begins when you've delivered the best possible version of your product with the best possible service. Your best will get better over time.

Zombie viruses are effective because of the ease with which they can be transmitted. The virus is a model of cost efficiency and the zombie virus in particular can be weaponized in short order because it exploits the fact that its hosts are social creatures that tend to congregate in population dense areas. No man is an island, especially not in the age of social media and instantaneous, ubiquitous communication.

As an artist seeking to lower operating costs, I settled upon the "art card" as the most easily transmittable format for sharing my work. An art card is a baseball card sized original work of art. Because of the ease of transport and convenience of storage, these are highly desirable and sought after by art collectors around the world. These are painted on 2.5"x3.5" surfaces, usually canvas, watercolor paper, or bristol board.

The marketing value of the art card can be understood in the context of the "free sample." The art card gives the collector a sense of an artist's style. These minor investments give the collector enough information to decide whether to invest in larger, more expensive pieces. For an author, the this might take the form of a free eBook, whereas filmmakers use trailers to promote their movies, and recording artists release singles. The concept here is to make it economically feasible for your intended customers to own what you are offering.

The "freemium" business model is another example of this principle. Software companies will often give a free version of the software to use, no strings attached. However, when the user wants to access more advanced features, the premium version of the software must be purchased. The value for the provider of the product is that the freeloaders are still submitting their email address, personal information, and are then added to a database of potential buyers.

Your product must be accessible if it is to become ubiquitous. It must exist in some unrestrainable form. Art cards, unlike large canvases, can be inexpensively submitted to galleries or potential collectors to make a greater impression than a mere website link to a portfolio. Every product you give away retains its value to you as a word of mouth marketing tool. The phenomenon of videos or Internet memes "going viral" is predicated on the public's unimpeded access to said meme or video. If people had to pay money to view funny cat videos then funny cat videos wouldn't take up the exorbitant levels of bandwidth they occupy now.

Art cards became a staple item for me because they were inexpensive to produce, cheap to ship, and easy to share. When was the last time you witnessed an original artwork being passed around a classroom or other social event? It tends not to happen because most artwork is not so readily transmittable. Whatever your product or service is, you must isolate some aspect of it which can be used to draw in new clients. Direct sales is inherently limited by the size of your sales force. With Zombie Marketing, you will use the phenomenon of people interacting socially to drive your sales, thereby making everybody a part of your sales force.

A musician could record a musical sample to be given away as a ringtone, and even though it's free, it could easily result in more actual sales than if it was being sold, even at a low price. This is because a catchy ringtone will attract attention, incite conversation, and introduce the music to new listeners. "Free" no longer constitutes a loss on the part of the seller because marketing is not a zero sum game. Attention itself has value, so seek to make your product, your brand, your song, or your book into the subject of conversation.

On one particularly slow day at a flea market, I radically dropped the prices of my artwork just to keep the product moving. Even though I lost money that day, one of those paintings later turned up in a private collection of art which included some very well known artists. One of those paintings, which I sold for five dollars, was displayed beside an original Picasso at a museum in Idaho. That is not something I could have predicted, or paid for, or otherwise coerced into happening. It was a byproduct of me not being an obstacle to the transmission of my product.

I give art cards away as free samples when I can afford to, or I at least make it possible for new buyers to obtain them for close to what I pay to ship them.The better deal the buyer gets, the more value you will have created for the buyer. The more value you create, the more inclined they will be to share their experience with those that they know. There have been times where I've sold art at a loss only to recoup those losses when the buyer returns for more art, or better yet, when they refer other potential buyers. People befriend other because of their common interests. Therefore, when you're selling a product or service to one person, it is reasonable to expect that their friends will be made aware of what it is you have to offer.

The primary strategy employed with Zombie Marketing is the implementation of cost-efficient methods for putting your product in the hands of potential buyers. Widespread brand awareness is the result of making your products visible, accessible, and sharable. Your revenue may not necessarily come first, nor will it always arrive directly, but it will come, presuming that your fan-base increases over time. Your revenue will increases as a natural response to the dynamics of supply and demand, both of which are factors you can directly influence.

13

Chapter 2. The Power of Replication

Zombies have undergone significant changes since their arrival in popular culture, but the essentials have remained the same. Technological improvements, new scientific advances, and geopolitical conflicts have served to make them more plausible, more entertaining, and more terrifying, but at the end of the day, a zombie is still just a zombie. So what is it that accounts for the unremitting consistency of the zombie throughout the last century and their increasing popularity in this one?

Is it their symbolic value as spectres of a more barbarous version of ourselves? Are they a reflection, as public intellectual Noam Chomsky speculated, of a deep-seated insecurity within the Western mind about the sustainability of post-industrial civilization itself?:

"My guess is that it's a reflection of fear and desperation. The United States is an unusually frightened country, and in such circumstances, people concoct, maybe for escape or relief, narratives in which terrible things happen." --- Noam Chomsky

My contention is that it's something far simpler. According to my analysis, the zombie's enduring popularity can be attributed to its design. The characteristics which make up a zombie are extremely easy to visualize, easy to replicate in costume, and since they have cultural counterparts in all societies, they cross all language barriers. Zombie films are inexpensive to make and zombies are generic in terms of ideology so they can be killed with impunity, making for perfect video game fodder. Zombies are living embodiments of death, which is something everyone fears, and they display the awesome destructive power of massive numbers of people working towards a common goal.

Many iterations of zombies have come and gone and yet the original design is still intact from movie to movie, book to book. Same monster, different scenarios, same enthusiastic audiences. Loyalty to the zombie as originally branded has allowed the niche to grow over time. Audiences forgive creative divergences from the original so long as the deviations don't contract the fundamental design. I cannot, at least not as I write this, imagine a zombie film in which the zombies sit down and have rational conversations with people, attempting to talk them out of their brains by winning them them over with logical debate. However, since brain eating undead creatures are still a part of it, the idea would probably take off.

The lesson here is that once you've isolated your niche there's no reason to deviate from what works as long as you're getting results. Standardizing your work will remove the random variables and aid in fine tuning your daily operations. Many of my initial mistakes pertained to the size of the art I was producing and selling. While I prefered to work large, it was clear that it was not economically feasible if my overall strategy was to sell far and wide. Size was the first constraint I had to learn to contend with. Despite the changes to the format of the work I sold, I didn't change anything else. My subject matter was consistent and I aimed for the same customer demographics. With your own products, once you've discovered your niche and your market, stay the course, and seek to grow your business by fine tuning your delivery.

By placing constraints on the fundamentals you'll actually have a lot more freedom to experiment with the details. For instance, if I stopped painting zombies and instead started painting pigs, then I'd be giving up a consistently growing market in favor an untested one. However, since I made the zombie theme work, I am free to experiment with variations on that theme without losing the momentum I've already established. In fact, I've sold several "zombie pigs". Standardizing your work doesn't mean that you sacrifice creativity. It only means that you channel that creativity into an effective catalyst for transmitting your product. A zombie virus can mutate and still spread, so long as it doesn't change into something for which we already have immunities built up.

The zombie themed art card became my staple money maker and marketing tool. By no means did I rule out other sizes or products, but these were my primary focus. At this phase, you need the single-mindedness of a ravenous zombie horde. If a horde deviated from its standard diet and instead went vegetarian, then the virus would die out. Sticking with a proven formula will allow you to streamline your processes and replace unproductive randomness with focused creativity.

Chapter 3: Real Time, Contact Time, and Dead Time

"Our days are identical suitcases---all the same size but some people can pack more into them than others."
---Anonymous

When I coordinate my time within the studio, I divide it into three categories: Real Time, Contact Time, and Dead time. Real Time refers to actual time while Contact Time refers to the amount of time I spend brush to canvas, in the act of producing a saleable piece. A typical work day might begin and end within a twelve hour window, but if only six of those hours are spent actually working, then for the purposes of organizing my production schedule, only the six of those hours count.

The purpose to this division is to eliminate waste. Streamlining your workflow is an ongoing effort to identify and eliminate waste. Since time is arguably your greatest resource, it is critical to invest it appropriately. If a six hour studio session involves work on a single painting, then it's probable that there will be some Dead Time within those six hours, for instance, time spent waiting for paint to dry. Less Contact Time relative to Real Time means less productivity. The objective is to bring these two measurements together, to make every minute count.

When I started the "1000 Zombies" series, the first thing I did was purchase a fan for my studio, and started working on multiple pieces at a time. The fan was used to speed up the drying process. By engaging in multiple paintings concurrently I discovered that I could get more Contact Time relative to Real Time.

Dead Time is when nothing is happening. Ignoring Dead Time is like ignoring loose nails on a boarded up window in the middle of a zombie occupied territory. The short periods of Dead Time are the easiest to ignore. I once had a roommate whose cat was in the habit of visiting me several times a day. If my door was closed, she'd open it, walk around, then exit, leaving the door open behind her. I got tired of having to continually re-close the door but did so without complaint. It was typical imperious cat behavior and I was used to it. But one day I realized that this seemingly innocuous interruption was costing me a break in concentration each time I put down the brushes to walk across the studio and push the door closed. I started keeping a yardstick within reach so that with my arm extended I could close the door behind the cat without the inconvenient waste of time.

"Big deal! It's only five seconds," some will say. To them I answer that yes, it is a big deal. Time is your greatest asset during the initial phases of your marketing strategy. Later, when you have transitioned from Micromanager to Macromanager, you'll have more flexibility with how you invest your time. .

Micromanaging your time will help you maximize the resources you have to work with so you can discard and minimize that which you can work without. It doesn't require a super detailed calendar. All it requires is a figure, a dollar amount, on what your time is worth, and then you'll have to start calculating this figure into how you ration out your time.

Establish what this figure is in terms of a basic fee or an hourly rate and then factor it into all of your decisions. For example, does it make more sense to order your supplies online or to save on shipping and make the purchases locally? Does it make sense to build a website yourself or to hire a designer?

Your prices may fluctuate a great deal or they might remain relatively static for long periods of time. What will change is your production rate. Even without painting faster, my own productivity increased with the application of these principles of time management.

On the basis of your observations, you'll be able to make changes to your processes which will make your time more effective. You must determine what your production quota is. My production quota consisted of the number of paintings I had to create and sell per week in order to keep the studio open.

Your quota will pertain to whatever it is that you're producing. When you set the quota, calculate for growth, not just breaking even. I call it "quota plus one". The "plus one" represents that which is above the bare minimum. It doesn't always mean extra work. It means you should allow time for investing into research, developing new ideas, and upgrading or refining your workspace.

Once you've determined your production quota, you can then make a calculation as to how much value each hour has for you. I must have a minimum of six hours per day, five days a week, in order to produce the amount of work to meet my requirements. In my case, this translates into fifty art cards per week at an average sale price of six dollars, for a total of three-hundred dollars per week. Divided into thirty hours of painting, I get a figure of ten dollars per hour as my hourly rate.

The hourly rate should be looked at as the amount it costs you per hour to not be working. So if you were to take time off for a dinner and a movie, you could see how the time away from your work has a dollar amount attached to it. It's important to have this as a baseline. When a person asks for a private commission I have to calculate how many studio hours it will take, and ascertain a price accordingly.

The purpose of having an accurate hourly rate is to avoid falling into the trap of under-charging for your work and under-valuing your time. Not charging enough to get the job done is like a cab driver not accounting for the cost of gasoline. Sure it's nice to offer low rates to family and friends, but those low rates come at a high price. This doesn't mean that you must give up on everything non-work related, but it is something which should be factored into your decisions both outside and inside of your work space..

The success of a zombie virus is predicated on the purposeful striving of its hosts. If zombies were ambiguous about getting their needs met; if they were lethargic in their pursuit of their next meal; or if they lacked the attention span required to focus on a single target long enough to catch it, their bodies would degrade and the virus would reach a dead end. But that's not how zombie are. Zombies are relentless, motivated, energized, and perpetually hungry.

You must incorporate the life-sustaining urgency of the zombie pack as it eats its way across the land, mindful of its purpose to the exclusion of all else. You'll have plenty of Dead Time....when you're dead.

Chapter 4: Getting Into Their Brains

There's an expression on the internet used to discourage unverifiable claims: "Pics or it didn't happen." Those words are the death knell to the braggart and they put an end to ridiculous chatroom confabulations. It's a silly meme but it underscores the importance of product photography. One of the easiest ways to ensure that your work is seen to take high quality photographs and plaster them onto the internet in such a way that web searches into your particular niche will bring your name brand to the forefront. No matter what your niche or product, the photographic evidence of its existence must be readily searchable.

Each photograph you upload to a blog or a website is just one more advertisement pointing back to you. The larger the collection of photographs you amass, the larger the net you can cast. High resolution images should be used whenever possible because if someone blogs about your brand or if a newspaper does a story on it, you'll want them to be able to print them.

You're wrong if you think that what you are doing has nothing to do with art or photography. The branding process is about searing your brand into the minds of those within reach. You must provide as immersive an experience as possible and since your first contact with your prospects will most likely be online, you need a visual presence.

If you're not particularly confident in your photography abilities or if you want to ensure that the images are of the highest quality, you can't go wrong with hiring a photographer. Find one that is building up their own portfolio so that their own self-promotion benefits you. Your zombie virus needs hosts to spread. Every person you employ is a carrier and transmitter for your brand. Thus, if you hire a photographer to do some promotional pictures for your product, encourage them to share the pictures on their own social media feeds. A competent and popular photographer will do more than just take pictures for you. He or she can carry your virus just as effectively as any fan or customer. Viral marketing strategies don't require the carrier's approval.

All of your photographs should be uploaded to your social media websites and #hashtagged appropriately. Facebook is free and allows you to store an unlimited amount of pictures in an organized fashion. Also, it has a download function should you ever want to have all your images located in a single compressed file. I frequently have buyers approach me for custom art after they come across an image I uploaded several years prior. Unlike time sensitive advertisements, your photographs will continue to attract buyers you long into the future.

Even if you're not an artist or graphic designer you'll should still endeavour to be artful and professional in how you present your brand. Try and recall your favorite album covers. Or is there a movie poster which captured your attention? Find an appealing aesthetic and commit to it. Observe how successful companies use technique this to build familiarity with their clients. Dress codes, uniforms, and "corporate culture" are what define a brand's personality.

Zombies, you may have noticed, all have the same personality, uniforms, and culture. You can spot on from a mile away. It's something about they way they walk and how they carry themselves. So to must your brand be recognizable from a glance.

If your product is music related or if you're a filmmaker or an author, the same principles still apply. If you do gangsta rap, you have to stay gangsta. If you're a heavy metal band, dress the part. If you deviate too much from your "front" or your projected image, can break the spell.

You have to define your brand. Don't leave it up to impersonal market forces or you'll go undefined, misrepresented, or possibly unnoticed. How many times have you seen a tabloid with an unflattering picture of an otherwise beautiful celebrity, caught on camera without makeup? There are some things which you cannot unsee. Be one of those things, but for reasons you decide.

Your goal is to achieve ubiquity by utilizing the interconnectedness of Web 2.0 and the seamless integration of social media with your real life interactions. No matter what you're producing, get in the habit of photographically documenting it. My web portfolios serve as catalogs. They serve as a public records of my progress and a convenient way to make my work instantly accessible. On every uploaded picture, I attach a link to the auction site that I use to sell my art. In this way, web searches which enter into the niche that I'm focused upon will bring new buyers who are merely one or two clicks away from making a purchase.

Product photography is critical to making an impression, especially if that product is yourself. Even a voice actor (who is mostly invisible) can benefit from a few headshots or a pictures sitting behind the microphone. Pictures of you "in action" are more relatable than text on an advertisement. The impression you make with your photography might be the only one needed to sell potential buyers on your brand.

Those who are sold on your brand will react favorable to seeing your products later, and won't need to be prompted into purchasing. There are no "impulse buys." People who buy something on impulse do so because they already know they want it. They are pre-sold. Most of us are pre-sold on candy, therefore, when we see candy at the checkout aisle at the grocery store, the buying decision is a no-brainer. If you've made the decision to purchase your product a "no-brainer", then you've successfully created a zombie for your brand.

I know a chef who Instagrams all of her desserts and now many thousands of people who have never tasted one of her creations are familiar with her brand. This means that her zombie virus has already been transmitted. If she ever decides to produce a national line of frozen desserts, she now has a built in customer base.

Uploading vast collections of properly hashtagged and keyworded images will make your brand stand out like a massive and inescapable wall of zombies. One or two might be easy to outrun or dodge, but mobbed together, there's no escape. You must have a presence on all the popular photo sharing blogs, social media sites, and print-on-demand websites. This is essential to making enough impressions on enough minds to break into the next phase: the onset of a pandemic.

Phase 1: Onset of a Pandemic.Morbidity in at Least One Segment of the Population.

Generating a Sales Contagion

Every horde begins with a single zombie, a "patient zero". Every plague has to start somewhere. One becomes two, two becomes four, four becomes sixteen, which becomes fifty, and fifty becomes one-thousand, and so on, exponentially. Whether or not that initial contagion spreads depends upon a number of factors, number one being the level of contagiousness and the proximity to a host with little to no immunity.

When an outbreak of zombieism infects the living, how far it travels and how deep it saturates the population is dependent upon numerous factors, not merely the size of the population. Other determining factors include terrain, defensive capabilities, climate, and individual susceptibility to infection.

The relative success a zombie horde has in subverting a human population is determined by many factors other than sheer numbers. Some may conclude that overwhelming numbers alone is a guarantor of success but that's a rather superficial analysis. For instance, a zombie horde could devour all the life within an area and find itself starving and confined to a limited geographical region. Without a route of transmission and the hosts to carry it, a horde could achieve impressive proportions but still starve and rot without ever leaving the city limits.

Zombie Marketing employs targeting the right niches while facilitating the expansion into new markets and demographics with a variety of tactics. If you were directing the spread of a weaponized zombie virus, you would have to target those hosts that are traveling away from ground zero into other population dense areas. This would mean you would target airports, bus stations, and truck stops. Numbers are important, for instance: web traffic. However, if the traffic isn't channeled properly, it may not move your virus out of Ground Zero.

It is often remarked---usually by salesmen--that "sales is a numbers game." Nothing could be further from the truth. Sales is not a numbers game. Such a haphazard approach treats the customers as interchangeable. Even with mass marketable products and services where there are vast numbers of customers, the companies that are best positioned and equipped will generate the most sales.

Previous to the Web 2.0 Revolution, big companies were in an advantageous position and could drown out the smaller competitors. Today, individuals can compete on a level playing field in what economist Thomas Friedman describes as the "flattening" of the world in his insightful book entitled The World is Flat.

Given this leveling of the playing field and the elimination of size as a major determinant factor in a product's success, the real focus now is on the merits of the product itself. Sales are determined more now than ever by the demonstrated worthiness of the product because instead of relying upon a big company's own ad copy and shilled customer reviews, there are community based rating systems which are inherently more honest because users are verified buyers. Presuming your product is of sufficient quality and your methods of delivery are effective, your sales will occur as a direct result of raising your brand awareness among your targeted demographics.

Unlike mass marketing, micro marketing pre-qualifies leads according to their interests. Instead of wasting effort on the disinterested, or the "immunized," Zombie Marketing efforts are directed at the specific niche, those who are susceptible to becoming hosts.

Mass marketing tactics reach out to cold leads, that is, leads that have not been prescreened according to individual preferences and likes. For instance, a mass marketing campaign might reach out to all women or all men. A micro marketing campaign, by contrast, might aim for individuals who like science-fiction books about alien octopuses mind-controlling our world leaders. The interconnectedness between providers of services and products with their potential customers has made it economically feasible to sell to small markets, whereas big stores cannot afford to give too much shelf space to products which only interest a tiny fraction of their customer base.

The goal is to sell products but the methods prescribed here are not about making sales pitches or cold calls. These methods of generating sales take indirect, sometimes guerilla approaches which seek to economize on effort. Each sale represents another success for your overall brand awareness and serves as an indication of how well your marketing strategy is paying off.

Making sales is the goal of your marketing strategy even if you're not selling physical or digital products. You're selling your brand, and this occurs in the minds of your customers. You can sell a lot of people on your brand for reasons unrelated to any particular product. You might find it helpful think of the zombie virus as a "mind virus." If you have ever heard a song you liked but didn't know the artist, then you know what it means to be pre-sold. If what you heard "hooked" you", then when you won't have to decide to buy the album or download the single when you see it advertised.

Target marketers are like snipers whereas mass marketers are less precise, wandering into hordes and firing at random. This only works if you have superior firepower and lots of ammunition. Otherwise, it's a suicidal and wasteful approach. As a target marketer, you must make every bullet count. Every effort must have an eventual payoff.

Consider direct mail campaigns, for example. Sending mail to new prospects, no matter how well researched those leads happen to be, will bring an average return on investment of less than 2 percent. It's a wasteful approach unless your advertising budget supports it, and even then you're still hemorrhaging money on the hopes of generating sales.

Now compare that with "Post Sale Marketing,"in which your advertisements are only directed to those who have either purchased from you in the past, or those who have subscribed to one of your social media accounts. The Zombie Marketing strategy focuses on these warm, or pre-qualified leads the way zombies focus on warm, living bodies.

There is an axiom taken from the movie Field of Dreams which says "if you build it, they will come." It's not quite a zombie flick but it is about dead baseball players coming back as ghosts. Unless you're dealing with the supernatural, that axiom won't serve you. Yes, you must build your "it", but you also must ensure there is a route in place so "they" can find it. In other words, having a great product and way to distribute it is only half the equation. The other half is putting your product into your prospect's field of awareness.

Like a contagion which requires close contact between the carrier and potential host, your products will sell close to one hundred percent of the time when you apply the tactics described in the following chapters. which focus on accurately identifying warm leads. Accurate targeting begins with identifying who and where your customers are, and how you can get to them.

Chapter 5: Target Rich Environments

According to the Urban Dictionary, a Target Rich Environment is a "combat situation in which an attacker, normally equipped with a superior weapons system, is presented with a large number of highly desireable, poorly defended and high-value targets all at once..."

To an encroaching horde of the recently zombified, there is nothing as nice as a population dense area, especially when it's a poorly defended one. In a similar vein, the target marketer must also seek popular places, going where the customers are, and having located them, he or she must know how to isolate the "high-value targets."

For a demonstration of this concept in practice, consider this example taking place in a shopping mall:

Susan, a salesperson selling purses from a kiosk, sees thousands of people a day pass through the mall. Her location is adjacent to the video game store which is next to the barber shop catering to men. Very few customers from the video game store or the barber shop take much of an interest in her purse display.

Obviously she's not immersed in a sea of high-value targets. While it is possible to pitch a sale to every passerby, no matter how good the pitch, few will be motivated to make a purchase if they haven't already had it in their minds to buy a purse. Even if one is great at making sales pitches, the process of facing dozens of rejections is not only tiring, but it's woefully ineffective. It's no better an approach than cold calling random numbers in the phone book.

Now, if Susan wants to exert more control over the rate of sales, she could relocate to the other side of the mall next to the women's shoe store which is adjacent to the place that sells beauty supplies. At this new location, even without making a strong effort to capture the attention of passerbys, she'll likely enjoy greater success because women who shop for beauty supplies and shoes are more likely to buy purses than men getting their beards trimmed or teenagers buying first-person shooters. She could probably just sit there reading a novel and operating the cash register, allowing the product to move itself.

So if your niche is purses, then you must move somewhere conducive to selling purses. By matching your niche to the appropriate Target Rich Environment, you take the guesswork and rejection out of sales and allow those high-value targets, those with their defenses down, to close the deal for you. The people in your niche are already pre-sold on the niche. There's no convincing necessary. Proper placement takes the selling out of sales and makes revenue generation a matter of strategy, not luck.

Long term dedication to a niche market will translate into brand differentiation. This can serve as your platform into larger markets. The idea is to become a big fish in a small pond first, then move into bigger pools. This is accomplished by aligning your niche with popular trends in order to bring in more customers. For instance, when I paint characters from The Walking Dead, I bring fans of the show into the Zombie Art niche. If I use the hashtag #TheWalkingDead on Twitter or Instagram, and I'm selling zombie themed products, then I am inserting my work into a Target Rich Environment.

A Target Rich Environment can be a geographical location, a certain hashtag feed, or it can be a moment in time. Black Friday, for example, is such a time. Holidays, sporting events, graduation ceremonies, are all occasions during which you'll have no trouble accessing high-value targets. Think of a ticket scalper outside of a major sporting event or popular rock concert. The scalper knows that his product is in the right place at the right time. Learn to think like a ticket scalper.

Cyclic trends are easy to follow, especially if you can attach your niche to holidays or specific anniversaries. For example, I have made it a tradition to paint Jason Voorhees, the undead psychopath from the movie series Friday the 13th, every time the thirteenth of the month appears on a Friday. Jason Voorhees is a type of zombie so fans of that movie franchise will often become collectors of my work. They find my work because they celebrate that character on those particular days and my paintings of him will show up under all the related hashtags. This puts my work in a Target Rich Environment.

Plan in advance to match your marketing efforts to related events and do it every time it comes around. Establish patterns and traditions to keep the same buyers in the loop, year after year. If you're in the business of selling floral arrangements, for instance, then you should be providing the Mother's Day gifts to the same homes year after year. Your clients should be prompted via email a month before Mother's Day to get their orders confirmed. If you don't prompt them early enough, they may find another florist. Too soon, and you're email will get lost in their inbox. If you time it right, you'll only have to send one email.

When you locate a Target Rich Environment, think like a sniper, not a mass marketer. Do your reconnaissance, set up ambushes, and endeavor to create situations favorable to a "one shot, one kill" success rate. Keep up with major events and holidays because even when you are established within a niche, you have to remain dedicated to earning the loyalty from your customers on a consistent basis. The nice thing about coordinating your marketing efforts with holidays, movie releases, or other large, target rich events is that you don't have to hunt down your targets. They come to you.

Chapter 6: Overcoming Resistance

As you may have noticed, zombies don't need to be sold on the benefits of consuming the brains, flesh, and viscera of the living. They don't have to be convinced or persuaded because the desire and need is already there, ingrained into their worldview. Their selection is made based upon which piece of meat is closer.

With regards to living consumers, the need to consume is likewise already there. The decision to buy is pre-existing and the only question is which particular good or service will best fill their needs. Often times, those decisions are not entirely rational. It could be as simple as the consumer likes the color blue more than the color red, or there could be more nuanced triggers driving those buying decisions.

When you're positioning your product in the marketplace, whether it is an obscure micromarket or a a something with mass appeal, you need a reason for buyers to look your way. Marketing is fundamentally about being noticed and when you've targeted the right customers they may look in your direction, but it's what you do with that attention that will close a sale.

Making a sale is a byproduct of properly directing the attention of your prospective buyers once you get it. The decision to choose a particular product may be emotion driven at its root but the decision to buy, to actually spend their money and invest in a product is an intellectual one. The rational side of the decision will cause second guessing and introspection. This is the part where the un-selling occurs. For instance, a buyer might be interested in a new t-shirt and find the design compelling and irresistible. However, when the time comes to enter their credit card information, other considerations become factors in the decision. Selling is about overriding that hesitation with clear reasons for closing the deal.

You have to be prepared to offer intellectual justifications for their impulse to buy. My experience in telemarketing taught me that if the potential buyer isn't hooked within the first few seconds, then no rebuttal will change their mind. If the prospect is willing to hear the entire sales pitch, then it generally means the person is looking for reasons to justify an impulse. Your pitch is where you give them reasons to say yes. The rebuttal is where you give them reasons not to say no. Even if the customer wants what you are offering, there may be other considerations they are taking into account.

Your sales strategy should aim at providing that slight nudge to finalize the transaction. Citing the existence of a money back guarantee is one such nudge which can influence customers teetering on the edge of a buying decision. Free shipping and handling is another reason for someone to say yes. The "freemium" business model is effective at making sales because there isn't really a sales pitch. It's more like a gift, and there is nothing disingenuous about it. The idea of reaching out with free samples is that you can show the customer that you are transparent in your intentions. You firmly believe that they will like what you are offering so much that they'll buy more later.

With Zombie Marketing, the "freemium" business model is preferred because even when a sale isn't made, the prospect still walks away with the product. Nobody says no to a free sample. In a way, the free sample is just a nice way of giving your prospects "an offer they cannot refuse." At that point it's up to your zombie virus to infect the host. You can allow them to say no to a purchase and rest assured that they'll be back if they truly like what you are offering. The sales tactics with Zombie Marketing are not aggressive or pushy, but rare actually quite passive and covert. Aggressive marketing is one thing. But when it comes to closing a sale, you have to let the virus do its work. Aggressiveness is off putting and besides, closing a sale should be about opening a door to a long term business relationship, not risking having that door slammed in your face.

High prices exclude people that cannot afford to pay. This sounds okay if you have buyers that are willing to pay high prices, however excluding those that cannot pay, or those who can but are unwilling to invest without knowing more, you're stifling the ability of those who were excluded to carry around your virus as hosts. Each buyer is valuable, even the ones who are shopping for good deals. A wealthy buyer is just as pleased to find a good deal as a person of modest income. However, both are likely to be repeat buyers if they are provided with a good product and excellent customer service. Everybody likes to be in on a good deal.

New iterations and improvements in your product will create repeat buyers. This is why it's critical that you think about customers as investors in your brand. You're not looking to take their money, but rather to give value for value. Your transactions must be win-win situations. Reciprocity has everything to do with growing a zombie horde. A zombie virus must be shared if it is to spread, and by offering good deals, you make your brand sharable.

Even if you have to lower your prices to drive sales up, remember that you're investing in a long term partnership with your buyers and they in you, therefore, consider that initial "loss" as a solid investment because you know they'll support the future editions and iterations of your product. A good sales strategy creates loyalties. You want converts. A zombie is good example of a convert. In fact, zombies are not only converts, but they are also evangelists. Seek to create brand evangelists. If you can gain more customers and move more products by lowering your prices, then you should because those buyers will not only be potential repeat buyers but will also serve as "electronic word of mouth" advertisers.

I have often distributed paintings to buyers at a loss, but treated it as an investment in advertising. If I sold a large painting and ended up losing money after paying for shipping, I would look at that loss, let's say ten dollars, and I would ask myself, "would I pay ten dollars to place this painting on a wall in someone's house on the other side of the country where it will be appreciated and talked about year round?" And my answer would invariably be yes.

With my auctions, I made buying decisions easy by starting with low prices and free shipping. Each bidder, even if they are bidding very low, has made the determination that they liked the art. The simple act of bidding is symbolic of an expressed desire. It also meant that they are either going to win or lose. They are no longer in neutral territory. This is analogous to the freemium strategy, in which the relationship is cemented, even if a sale isn't immediately forthcoming. Zombie Marketing is all about establishing that relationship that contact. Once you get that, the sales will follow. Zombie viruses take a few seconds, others take a few days, but in either case, if they came into contact with it, they'll turn eventually.

I occasionally auction items beginning with a one cent starting bid because it draws the biggest crowd. It's better to have one winner and twenty losers than two bidders resulting in one winner and one loser. The reason is that the twenty losers constitute a larger marketing force than one. They also serve to guarantee another dozen or more sales in the future.

The best way to spread the zombie infection to the largest number of people is to unleash it in a crowded place. Zombie Marketing isn't about generating isolated, one on one sales. It's about creating Sales Contagions which move across a population like a plague while you relax in the comfort of your Zombie Virus Laboratory at Ground Zero.

Chapter 7: Closing in for The Kill

You close sales by proffering compelling reasons to invest while removing barriers and obstacles. Zombies, like all predators, naturally economize on their energy. They go for the easy meat, that which is accessible. Once a horde has surrounded a home there is still the matter of entering. There may be significant fortifications between the zombies and the grey matter they crave. Are the windows boarded up? Are the doors blockaded? Overcoming resistance entails an understanding of what kinds of barriers prevent sales from closing. The obvious one is price, but there are other, less obvious ones to consider.

For instance, time. The longer a horde takes to get past the white picket fence, the more likely the resistance will stop the onslaught. A good deal will be passed over if it entails a complicated sign up process. Thankfully the ubiquity of social media has made signing up for online retails just a matter of a few clicks. The objective here is to streamline the method of sale as much as possible.

It only takes a few seconds for a living person to escape a zombie onslaught. In sales, every second counts. The rule I lived by when I was a telemarketer was the "three-second rule." The first three seconds of a phone call would determine how, or if, the next thirty seconds would proceed. If I lost their interest in the first three, then I wouldn't get the next thirty; and if those next thirty failed to create value for the prospect, then I'd lose the call. Wasted time can unseal the deal.

Another is hidden barrier is effort: the sheer amount of energy it takes to chase down a meal will affect whether or not a particular target will even be pursued in favor of less problematic options. Your marketing efforts will only succeed if your brand is easily accessible to your targeted demographics. Closing a sale, like closing in for a kill, is nine parts planning, one part execution.

Watch a lioness eat a gazelle and you'll see what I mean. There's nothing random about sales and it's not a numbers game. If it were, then the lionesses would just run out into a herd of prey animals and start biting and clawing, but that's not what they do. The lionesses approach is measured, calm, and it economizes on energy. When it moves in for the kill, it positions itself so there are no obstacles between its slavering jaws and the warm meal ahead. When it closes the deal, it does so swiftly, efficiently, and ruthlessly.

Here are examples of two different radio advertisements. Think of how they sound from a buyer's perspective:

1) "Hi. My website is H-T-T-P SLASH SLASH , DOT, W-W-W super marketing tactics dot com. You can go there and read all about it by clicking on the 'about' page, and then use the contact form there to share your email with me and from there you can subscribe to the newsletter."

and

2) "Hi. You can like my page at Facebook slash Bob's Burger Shack and follow my updates."

The first advertisement requires the listener to have a pen and scratch pad handy, and then it still requires additional follow up. The second one goes right for the throat.

Phase 2:Outbreaks and Epidemics in Multiple Countries

World Zombification

World Zombification is the goal of the zombie virus. In sales, this is called market dominance. Market dominance is measured by the extent to which a brand defines a particular market. A single zombie shambling down the street would hardly pose a threat to anyone. Outside the context of a zombie apocalypse, it would be treated as a mere curiosity, probably injected with thorazine and confined to a padded cell, with no one the wiser. There would be no hysterical headlines, no riots, and no social media frenzy (unless bath salts are involved *).

With zombies, their strength lies in numbers and in the fact that they don't have central authorities or a hierarchy, but rather they function as a leaderless insurrection, each acting independently, but all serving the same cause. This is the same structure used in guerilla warfare, where the structure of rank and file is jettisoned in favor of independent terrorist cells, united in ideology or common goal, but without the need for orders or directives from above. A leaderless resistance lacks a discernable head, or in the case of the zombie horde, a discernable brain.

The Zombie Marketing Strategy scraps conventional marketing tactics in favor of the more adaptable guerilla methods. Once a market is penetrated, the object is to saturate it with your brand, your own strain of zombie virus, until no potential host remains unexposed to it.

* *(South Beach Zombie reference)*

Chapter 8. Going Viral

The phenomenon of "going viral" appears random, capricious, and unpredictable. It is all of these things, however, it exactly doesn't occur in a vacuum. There must be a confluence of factors, such as audience receptivity, the relevance or quality of that which goes viral, and its means of transmission. While it may be a contradiction in terms to say one can plan to do something spontaneous, there are ways one can create circumstances favorable to the spontaneous occurring.

For an example of contrived spontaneity, let's look at the phenomenon of "guerilla art". These are examples of art outside of the traditional confines of a gallery, occupying the public space in some unapproved way. Vandalism comes to mind, but paradoxically, it's a form of vandalism which can be quite pleasing to the eye and artistically provocative. Guerilla art doesn't ask permission, and its anonymity makes it mysterious. Add to that the daring and boldness of the deed itself, the deliberate defacing of property in the public space, and you're left with something which is more remarkable than it would be in any other context.

Guerilla art bypasses all the usual filters between the artist and the public. It recontextualizes the art and permits the immediacy of a direct experience outside the contrivances of a gallery. At best, guerilla art is appreciated based upon its merit. At worst, it's derided as graffiti, if not ignored entirely. The purpose of guerilla art is to entertain, to bemuse, to shock, and to provoke. The act of placing a work of art in a public place is an act of defiance. Some works will incite outrage while others will garner wide-spread approval. The point is, guerilla art elicits spontaneous reactions in those that encounter it.

If you take on the mindset of a guerilla artist, you'll get an idea of how to attract attention. It doesn't have to be in a shocking questionable manner. It simply has to be engaging enough to trigger a response worthy of a social media mention. Whether or not something goes viral is a matter of opportunity, of being in the right place at the right time with the right message. Some would say luck, but luck, as the Roman philosopher Seneca said "is what happens when preparation meets opportunity."

Zombie Marketing is not just about being prepared for a zombie apocalypse: it's about creating opportune conditions for one to occur. Nothing goes viral by accident. It may not be deliberately contrived but it's still not an accident. Something goes viral when it's eminently shareable. This can be for good reason, bad reasons, stupid reasons, it doesn't really matter what it is, so long as it has a receptive audience.

Here are some examples of situations which have viral marketing potential:

1) **Hoaxes**--- For hoaxes to work, you have to engage the news media. It will also help to have someone to act as a bystander and help to direct the crowd's attention. If you owned a company that designed and sold unmanned aerial drones, you could stage a UFO hoax. You would have to do little more than launch one which has been fitted with bright lights after the sun has gone down. You and your assistants would then call the news media from separate phone numbers. You would snap photos and post them on Instagram, Twitter, and put video footage on Youtube. Later, you could reveal the hoax--once you've garnered enough attention. Hopefully you can make it on the evening news.

2) **Smart Mobs**--- Use social media to organize a smart mob and have the mob incorporate your product into their act. For example, if you sold your own line of yoga related products, you could stage a "yoga in", where several dozen or more more of your customers, incentivized with free or discounted product, show up at a shopping mall food court at a designated time, and when given the signal, they all roll out their yoga mats on top of their tables, climb on top, assume a lotus flower position, and begin chanting "Om" in unison. Eventually, the word would get out that it was staged by your company.

3) **Pranks**--- The best pranks are those which don't make fools out of the targets but rather include them in the laughs. Hell Baby is a horror comedy movie which was made massively popular by a prank played on pedestrians. It involved a remote controlled baby stroller with an animatronic devil baby inside. People walking by would hear a baby crying and upon seeing an apparently abandoned stroller would get up close to it, at which point the Hell Baby would sit up and screech. Then the stroller would roll

away on its own. People screamed, then laughed hysterically. The video of the prank received tens of millions of hits even before the movie hit the theatres.

4) **Crowd Sourced Content**--- You can organize contests which require users to submit their own content. For example, if you were in the business of selling clothes for pets, you could offer prizes for best dressed cat or dog. The only requirement would be that they are wear your brand of pet clothing.. The contestants would submit photographs of their pets to your website where winners would be selected via an online poll. You could offer gift cards, cash prizes, or free product. The point is, each contestant would spend five or ten dollars on your brand just to enter the contest. Whether or not one of the entries goes viral, you would still draw a huge crowd and generate significant revenue in the process.

Chapter 9: Something to Scream About

When a ragged, rotting, gore-soaked mass of the walking dead comes marching down your street, your natural impulse will be to warn everyone around you. There isn't any need for the horde to beg you to tell everyone of their arrival. The situation is eminently shareable, hash-taggable, and worthy of people's' attention.

Your product must speak for itself. If it's noteworthy, it will be noted. You can get people to talk about your brand and share it simply by place it where people are already discussing it, or something like it. This is how contextual advertising works. An advertiser purchases ads according to the keywords and metadata of the websites where it will be displayed. The Internet is home to millions of and millions of conversations. People are already talking. Your objective needs to be to get your brand to become the subject of those conversations.

Word of mouth is widely accepted as the best form of advertising money can't buy. This is true, yet there are still ways you can predictably generate it. The typical approach to advertising usually includes the purchase of advertising space or air time. This investment may or may not attract attention, and even if the attention is held, it may not lead to sales. It's not an exact science, but it works well when the lead pool is filtered. The use of keywords, or tags, combined with other demographical options, such as age or personal interests, ensure that your advertisements are placed in front of potential buyers.

Consider the expense of a billboard. The price is going to be relative to its size, location, and length of time it will be displayed. The gamble is that the sheer number of drivers passing by will generate enough leads and sales to compensate for the cost of the signage. But even if the traffic exceeds the best estimates, there's no guarantee that drivers are actually discussing or thinking of whatever the sign advertises. This is just the nature of treating sales and marketing as a numbers game.

So where do you find these conversations into which you can interject your zombie virus? Where can you find real time conversation on any topic at any time? The blogosphere is one place to find dialogue, but blogs are not real time conversations. They are polished, edited, and published first, then the readers can interact in the comment sections. Real time blogging does exist, but not in the blogosphere--it's in the micro-blogosphere---most famously, the Twittersphere.

You may not have been among the first to jump into micro-blogging. You may have ridiculed Twitter and those that Tweet, perhaps thinking it was a fad. But nobody can deny the power of marketing via micro-blogs and images sharing websites.

If you text message people then you're no different than a Tweeter. The difference is that Twitter creates a publically accessible feed and opens you to legions of other users. There's nothing trite or faddish about it. Tweeting is just a modern form of the telegraph. As dumb as a the jargon may sound, the social realities of the day are what they are. Microblogging is about saying as much as possible with the least amount of characters.

Each Tweet or other microblog post serves as an advertisement for something, some idea, person, or thing. For the niche marketer, Twitter is a dream come true and here's why: blogs and websites are isolated entities. While they may in fact be instantaneously accessible, their interconnectivity with other blogs and websites is dependent upon searchers seeking them out. Microblogging, whether by Twitter or similar websites, puts all its users together in one forum.

Think of your blog or portfolio as a store and your microblog as a kiosk at the local shopping mall. The kiosk gets the walk by traffic and if you're positioned by the correct stores, you'll benefit from the cross marketing. If someone likes your products at the kiosk then you can refer them to your store.

Microblogging has effectively merged the personal with the social in a free market of ideas which places no barriers on admission and imposes no limits on one's popularity. By merit, luck, or happy accident, one's Twitter account may earn the favor of enough followers to draw in a constant influx of relevant traffic.

The focus of each Twitter or Instagram post should be to draw a crowd. Your microblogging accounts serve as portfolios, showcasing your products. My own twitter account has thousands of my paintings chronicled. If something I post gets a Retweet, it draws people in who might otherwise have never heard of my work.

For the purposes of hotlinking to your products, choose a domain name that is simple, concise, and memorable. This domain name is part of your branding so name it appropriately. It's going to be used for business cards, email footers, and when referring people via word of mouth. Ideally, the domain name will match the keywords and hashtags you use when promoting your work.

For example, JanesButteflyArt.com and BobsLandscapery.com align with their particular niches. Here's how it worked for me. Right now, if I search for "Zombie Art" on the Google, out of all the instances of that phrase being used, my portfolio usually shows in with the top ten positions, and many of my paintings are readily visible. Each one, wherever it is found, whether a blog or an auction or a social media post, contains the same keywords, "Zombie Art" and places the viewer just a few clicks--or taps--away from a purchase. All my social media names use the same keywords, i.e. Twitter.com/ZombieArt and Facebook.com/ZombieArt.

Marketing on microblogging platforms requires that you contribute regularly to your area of interest. Engage in conversations and without even asking them to, other users will look at your profile page, see what you're about, and have your website link readily available should they choose to interact further.

Chapter 10: Widespread Contamination

Now here's something which may go against common wisdom: I don't believe in hoarding the art or controlling access to the images. Instead, I freely disseminate them by posting to several sets of blogs and social media accounts. Every time I list a painting on an auction, I post pictures in as many places as possible, giving each one it's own blog post. The purpose is to extend the usefulness and value of each piece indefinitely. Thus, a painting sold today will continue to exist as a publicly displayed work and a permanent record of the date of creation, and it will contain links to my present work.

This allows potential collectors to observe the development, the history, and the iterations my work has undergone in the interim, and thus they can make additional assessments about whether or not to invest. Whatever your product is, there needs to be evidence of it, blogs posts about it, forums about it, and there should be audio or video content available, complete with links to your store.

The key concept here is what I call the Decentralized Web Presence. The Decentralized Web Presence is an approach for search engine optimization and niche marketing. The idea is that instead of concentrating your presence in a single location or website over which you have total control, you instead focus your efforts on casting as wide a net as possible. You want your customers to find your brand even if they don't know it exists. You want to "contaminate" every related hashtag and web forum related to it with images or postings which point back to your product or service.

Zombies are often observed apparently sending scouts. Whether it's a hunting instinct akin to what ants do or whether it's just them stumbling about, the point is, they will venture far and wide so as to not miss a single brain. Similarly, the tactic in Zombie Marketing is to place your brand where your customers go and spread out from there, saturating the area, making your presence impossible to miss.

"Location, location, location" is an expression well known to real estate agents and store owners. This bit of wisdom holds that the main factor determining whether a business succeeds or fails is its location. The same expression applies to online marketing. Instead of thinking of locations as geographic areas, you're thinking in terms of online searchability within those places where your target market groups interact with one another.

A Decentralized Web Presence serves many purposes and doesn't take as much times as you might think. Most blogs and social media sites give you the option of posting by email or sharing content across various platforms simultaneously. This means that you can post to several blogs at once. When I share my artwork in this manner, it is similar to a press release for each piece, and the keywords and titles are always directed appropriately.

Author Brian Kaufman did a web search of "zombie art" , found me, and shortly thereafter commissioned cover artwork for his zombie novel "Dead Beyond The Fence: A Novel of the Zombie Apocalypse.":

If I had not been focusing my work into a niche, then his search might not have given priority to my particular brand of zombie art. As an added bonus, the author's existing readership was introduced to my work. The nice thing is, he can sell thousands of books faster than I can produce thousands of paintings. That's the level of targeted marketing which you must strive for.

Observe "Rules For The Internet # 198" which states that "if it's not on Google, It does not exist. No Exceptions." By spreading your contamination across different social media platforms and websites your brand will be visible, searchable, downloadable, and ultimately purchasable. In a word: infectious.

Chapter 11: Cross Contamination

Cross Contamination Marketing is a calculated way of inserting your product into unrelated markets at opportune times. Holidays, sporting events, elections, music festivals, are all opportune times for reaching new demographics.

This works when you can align your product or service with a pre-existing demand and insert it into the area where the most excitement or buzz is located. Here's a simple example: selling bottled water at a crowded outdoor event. It would be better still if your logo and QR code were on those water bottles.

The idea is that you're reaching outside of your target market at a time and place where you are guaranteed sales. In other words, you're selling to individuals who are already pre-sold. As with all the marketing tactics you employ, the basic concept is to provide value to the customer.

The creation of value is critical because you're goal is to create a long term relationship with your customers. You want to count on their loyalty with every new iteration of your product. You'll want them referring you to their friends, and their friends to theirs.

A Zombie Virus doesn't just make someone sick and turn them for a day. It changes them completely. There is no turning back. This is how effective marketing should work. It should create converts to your brand.

One way to find these opportune times and places is to research popular news sites and following the latest "trending topics" on your favorite search engine. Use your calendar application and have reminder emails sent to yourself regarding upcoming holidays. I like to paint Zombified Christmas elves each year but if I don't have them ready to sell by mid-December I will miss my window of opportunity.

Here's a short list of successes I have had with Cross Contamination Marketing:

1. Miley Cyrus-- I painted Miley with her tongue hanging out the week of her infamous MTV "twerking" performance. It sold for $198.00. At any other time, it would have sold for $20, no more. The popularity of the piece had to do with people on Twitter sharing the image with their followers. The buzz around that event drew in bidders who had never heard of my work.

2. Twinkie Zombie -- When Hostess announced it was closing, I purchased several dozen boxes of Twinkies and other snack items to sell at an inflated price on Ebay. Additionally, I kept the packaging from a box of Twinkies I myself consumed and painted the mascot into a Zombie Twinkie. It attracted lots of hits and outsold my conventional zombies.

3. Serial Killers -- Selling paintings of serial killers draws in significantly greater traffic than what my usual art attracts. This applies to real life serial killers and movie villains. Many of those who examine the serial killer art, or "murderabilia", are intrigued by my other art and remain long term buyers.

4. Celebrities -- Any popular celebrity will have their built in public relations and marketing efforts. All you have to do is promote your work on their social network pages and fan sites and you'll garner attention. I have often tapped into new markets by doing paintings of celebrities or famous athletes. Cameo appearances, it should be mentioned, are a form Cross Contamination Marketing. These are publicity stunts where an actor, celebrity, or politician can boost their brand awareness by appearing on a movie or television show as an unofficial guest.

5. Jason Voorhees-- Every Friday the 13th, I take advantage of the predictable Internet buzz and I paint the machete wielding movie villain. It's one of my more popular ongoing series,and my auctions honoring the horror-holiday have become a tradition of mine. Every fan of Jason Voorhees is a zombie art fan whether they know it or not; my job as a marketer is to let them know.

It's helpful to use Venn diagrams to map out your customers by their market groups and look for overlaps. The areas of overlapping interests is where you cross contaminate. In addition to zombies, cats have always sold well for me. Now, while cat people aren't always zombie fans, zombie fans are always cat people. At least according to my own results.This means that I can sell cats to cat people and it won't alienate my zombie art collectors. When I paint Zombie Cats, it merges the two groups of collectors. Properly executed, Cross Contamination Marketing is an effective way to build bridges between disparate groups of customers.

Chapter 12: Memetic Engineering

A meme is a unit of cultural information, like an idea, an image, or a phrase. Memes are analogous to genes, and are used to understand the transmission of ideas through a society in much the way that genetics studies how genes move through populations.

Memetic Engineering isn't about breeding hybrid science fiction monstrosities and loosing them upon civilian populations. We'll leave that to the genetic engineers. Memetic Engineering is about creating unique combinations and juxtapositions of popular memes, and presenting them in new, and hopefully transmissible forms. A properly constructed meme, or meme-complex, will replicate itself endlessly, and in doing so will increase the prevalence of your brand.

Memetic Engineering is a method of cross pollinating ideas until a combination finds hosts in previously uninfected demographics. As I described in the previous chapter, I've found that a disproportionately high number of cat people are also zombie connoisseurs. Therefore, when I started painting cats, most of the buyers crossed over. Then, when I started painting Zombie Cats, something new happened. This meme-complex commanded higher prices than either zombies or cats alone. This was a product of the increased number of bidders from two overlapping demographics.

In October of 2012 I created a zombie sculpture and fashioned it in the likeness of Anderson Cooper, a well-known journalist and television personality. Television news anchors are more than teleprompter reading talking heads. Today more than ever they are part of the news. They are distinct personages and have their own loyal fans. So when I appropriated the unit of cultural information that is "Anderson Cooper" the brand and mixed it with my "Zombie Doll" which is itself a mixed meme, I had something which targeted four demographics:

1. People who collect handmade dolls.
2. People who like zombies.
3. Fans of Anderson Cooper
4. Anti-fans of Anderson Cooper

When I released the Anderson Cooper Zombie Doll on Ebay, Facebook, and Twitter, it was widely shared and commented on. Someone posted it on Anderson Cooper's Twitter hashtag #andersoncooperlive. This brought it to the attention of his staff, who found it amusing.

Mr. Cooper found it worrisome because at the time he was contending with a stalker. He thought the bloody doll with his face was a potential death threat. His personal assistant contacted me to see if I was crazy or just creative (or both).

After we spoke I was invited onto the show for one of its more lighthearted segments. It didn't pan out because the show underwent some changes and dropped the segment, but it demonstrated to me the power of Memetic Engineering and targeted mixed-meme dissemination.

Mixing memes is an effective way to cross-market and expand your overall base of repeat customers. This is especially true when what you introduce coincides with a preexisting media frenzy or trend. The key is experimentation. You must venture into new territory and this means you'll have to expect a few chimeric monstrosities to arise on your way to finding the right hybridization.

Android + Zombie = A design which appeals to horror fans, science fiction buffs, and computer geeks.

Phase 3: End of the First Pandemic Wave

What We Can Learn From The Survivors

The hypothetical zombification of a nation, while not exactly a desirable future, can teach us a lot about marketing. But proper market research must also take into account the perspectives of those outside of the targeted demographics. No epidemiological study would be complete without assessing the entire population, including the survivors.

From the perspective of the living, zombies are notoriously dumb, clumsy, and if the definition of insanity is failing the same way over and over, then they're insane as well. The advantage they do have is sheer numbers, which the living can counter by using their brains to act and strategize. This, however, is only possible when fear has been overcome. Fear paralyzes rational thought and rational thought is the key to outsmarting a horde of cannibalistic killers.

The legendary stupidity of the zombie mob stems from its short-sightedness and its range of the moment mentality which does not ration nor produce, but only mindlessly consumes. So the first thing which the living can teach us then, is that survival depends upon planning ahead and seeing beyond the next meal. To avoid doing so is to risk becoming someone's next meal. Planning ahead is all about setting expectations and making reasonable assumptions.

Even if survival seems unlikely, the necessary attitude is a hopeful, optimistic, goal oriented one. This is not a detachment from the facts of reality, but an unwavering self-confidence in the face of overwhelming odds. Attitudes, positive or negative, create self-fulfilling prophecies, so you'll be better off adopting a positive outlook. Robert Neville in the book I Am Legend was literally the last man on Earth. He didn't give in to hopelessness or despair but instead spent his time constructively seeking a cure for the zombie virus which had turned the entire world against him.

Chapter 13: Leaders vs. Naysayers

"Keep away from people who try to belittle your ambitions. Small people always do that, but the really great make you feel that you, too, can become great."" --Mark Twain

There are two kinds of people every entrepreneur must be able to identify: Leaders and Naysayers. Leaders are the teachers, guides, trailblazers, and successful entrepreneurs who set examples for others to follow. Naysayers, also known as haters, do the exact opposite of what Leaders do, making it their life's purpose to stifle creative risk taking before it moves beyond the idea phase.

Both types will seem genuinely interested in your success. Naysayers want to be there if your plans fail so they can do a "see I told you so" and enjoy their moment of schadenfreude. Leaders, by contrast, don't criticise failure unless it's in a constructive manner. This is because Leaders know that all successes arise when failure is strategically confronted and overcome, each failure representing another stepping stone on the path to mastery. A Leader will share in your vision of a better future and encourage your progress.

Naysayers never attempt anything so they never learn to fail properly. No one learns to walk without learning to fall. When toddlers are taking their first steps, they are coached and encouraged, not mocked and discouraged. The Naysayer will shoot down your vision of a better future, and will instead judge your present solely upon your past failures. They use ridicule and sarcasm to invalidate any part of you which doesn't conform to their own limited vision of who you are, a mold they dissuade you from breaking.

The essential difference between the two relates to their psychological response to the emotion of envy. Envy is a raw, painful emotion that one feels when their own perceived inferiority or shortcomings are brought to the surface by the appearance of another who possesses superior qualities. It's a childish emotion, and in the mature mind it manifests as a capacity to admire the achievements of others. Those who are capable of admiring and appreciating others are also capable of emulating and learning from others.

An envious mind, however, resists learning from the targets of their hatred--and hatred is what it is. Envy is a covert, sublimated hatred which expresses itself with a sneer, a sarcastic retort, and passive aggressiveness. For an envious person to learn from the envied is to admit a perceived personal deficiency. Think about Snow White and the Seven Dwarves: the Evil Queen couldn't stand the idea of a more beautiful person than herself, so rather than celebrating diverse expressions of beauty, she sought to have Snow White brutally murdered.

Much of the storyline within The Walking Dead has as much to do with interpersonal drama and power plays as it does with the humans versus zombie scenario. Zombies are united in undeath whereas the living are internally divided in a myriad of ways. This means that Leaders must learn to discern the Naysayers and haters in their own camps in order to maintain an effective front against the enemy without.

Once You've Identified Them:

Focus on the Leaders in your field. Subscribe to their social media networks, watch their videos, read their blogs and books. By constantly immersing yourself in the experiences of the successful, you'll inoculate yourself against the subtle demoralizing effects of the haters, overt or covert.

Since Naysayers are unavoidable, there are some useful rules of thumb to adhere to. For instance, it's often wise to do the opposite of what the Naysayers suggest. It can be valuable to examine what the Naysayers are telling you if you can keep in mind the premises their opinions rest. Naysayers often reflect conventional ways of doing things, so if they think an idea is particularly good, you might be well served to cross that off your list of ideas to pursue. Their feedback, however poisonous, can be a barometer, indicating when you're really onto something good.

No other factor in your life can have as detrimental an effect upon your work than the Naysayer. They actively seek to destroy or suppress that which they envy. It's not that they want what is yours; they just don't want you to have it.

The most difficult thing about them is their covert, subtle means of undermining and invalidating the efforts of others. They will turn your confidence into self doubt, your ambition into shame, and will tear down your self-esteem until you cease to produce---if you let them. They will attempt to coerce you into seeing failure as a reason to stop. In the Zombie Apocalypse, these are the ones who see no reason left to go on just because things appear bleak at the moment.

Maybe you're in a supportive environment, but this doesn't mean that someone close to you isn't working surreptitiously against you. You must be on the lookout for envy because it rarely comes out in the open. Envy is not really a green eyed monster; it's a snake in the grass; a knife poised to strike you in the back; and it lurks behind friendly facades which it uses to get close enough to do damage.

Subjective opinions should be ignored in favor of the one objective measure you have for gauging your progress, and that is your performance in the marketplace. The marketplace has no ulterior motives and its judgements are impartial and fair. Pay attention to yourself, those you deem Leaders, and the marketplace.

According to Napoleon Bonaparte,"the greatest emperors crown themselves." This is because consensus opinion does not make you what you are, you do. Therefore, it's up to you to stake your claim. Naysayers will always ask you, "who do you think you are?" Leaders will say, "crown thyself."

Chapter 14: Surviving the Siege

In many ways, managing a successful business is like surviving a zombie siege. There may be no end in sight, just an unwavering objective to survive and thrive under circumstances in which the enemy is relentless and overwhelming. Day to day existence requires precise resource management, standardized operating procedures, and constant innovation with the aim of establishing secure, long term survival. The bare minimum for daily survival includes patrolling the premises, checking for weak spots in your defenses, and acquiring new sources of raw materials.

Then there's the question of forming a band or going solo. Will you remain a sole proprietorship or incorporate? Every entrepreneur is a solitary monopolist. To the extent in which one works within a group framework, the individual power is dispersed. You could wind up in a mutually dependent relationship with potentially unreliable, unscrupulous, or incompetent individuals who aren't as concerned with your survival as you are. Remember, nobody starts out as a zombie. Even the best of friends can turn, so it may be advisable not to share your power.

Group dynamics can be inimical to individual self-interest and self-expression. The very tribal nature of the social dynamic requires a degree of self-sacrifice and compromise. Then there's the questions of money, credit, branding, resources, responsibility, variable skills, strengths, and weaknesses.

It takes more than merely holding your ground each day if you wish to eventually declare victory. You're either moving forward or you're falling behind. There's no middle-ground when you're under siege. There must be constant pushback on your part. It's a war of attrition..Your defenses must be reinforced and improved constantly. What happens when a zombie breaks through a barrier and you lack the nails to board it back up? You must do all that you can and then some. The situation may not be always be ideal but as long as you stay in the fight, sooner or later, you'll have a break-through.

Remember: lots of guts, lots of glory. Entrepreneurism is for risk takers, for those individuals who take responsibility for themselves. Should you take those risks, meet those challenges, and fend off those hordes, then you might wake up one day and see nothing but bones littering the now quiet streets surrounding your fortress. This would be the point where your business goes from surviving to thriving.

Chapter 15: Rise Above The Crowd

"Death is nothing, but to live defeated is to die every day." --Napoleon Bonaparte

The most commonly depicted approach to surviving the zombie apocalypse. In film and literature is the defensive posture, where the living attempt to establish a stable and defensible position. It is probably the most rational in most circumstances. It's analogous to the individual who does things the way they have always been done. The idea isn't so much to win as to maintain. It's about achieving an acceptable status quo.

The second method is to engage the hordes head on, to fight against impossible odds. This one analogous to the entrepreneur who charges head on into the action without regard to convention or orthodoxy. This method is all about eliminating the win. It's a win or die tryin approach but it promises a better future than the acceptable status quo of the first option.

The Zombie Marketing strategy partakes of both methods. This strategy is exemplified in the novel I Am Legend, by Richard Matheson. It's about Robert Neville, the last living man on Earth, and his one man war against a zombified world. He maintained a fortified home by night and by day he hunts and kills off the zombies as they sleep. (Matheson's zombies shared many characteristics of vampires in this novel and can't stand the light of the sun.)

Robert Neville was actively seeking a cure for the devastating disease and he spent his time researching and experimenting, hoping to find a way to get the world back to the way it was.The plan eventually fails as he's overrun and the world is entirely converted to the the undead. However, despite losing the war, he takes satisfaction in knowing that he will survive in legend, as a sort of inverted Dracula myth. Robert Neville achieved market distinction.

To achieve market distinction, one must be prepared to reject the herd mentality and to face the consequences of doing so. If there's one thing a herd does not like, it's rejection. All groups have ways of punishing the apostate, the ones that chose to self-exile, to differentiate.

Zombies eat the living; it's just the natural order of things. Self-confidence and blinding optimism will make you a target of naysayers and haters. This too is just the natural order of things. But if you truly believe in what you are doing, then the opinions of others should not matter. However, before you reveal yourself as un-zombified fresh meat, there are a few preparations you must make.

First, you must have your fortifications built. If your goal is to achieve brand differentiation then you have to be ready for what comes when you do. There's a well known Japanese proverb which is applicable to your quest for market distinction: "the nail that sticks out shall be hammered down."

The zombies will come whether you're ready or not. Once you stand out from the masses and show that you're a unique, living and breathing army-of-one, they will come for you. You must prepare for the opposition and understand that no matter how innocuous and peace loving you happen to be, you simply cannot survive in the zombie apocalypse of a competitive economy without adopting a more warlike attitude

Your originality will draw them to you like scavenging ghouls, for good ideas only arise in functioning brains---the kinds of brains that make zombies salivate. They can smell the neocortex of an idea-person or an entrepreneur from a mile away. Their attacks are often enough to cause most ideas to disappear as the originators to succumb to the horde and merge with the walking brain dead.

I have long since lost count of how many times I've been told to stop painting zombies. People would politely ask me why I don't just paint fruit baskets and landscapes. The implication was that there was something wrong with me, that I had deviated from the herd and therefore needed to be guided back to it. In fact, I started painting again in 2009 after a ten year hiatus--because I had just taken it for granted that my work was not acceptable.

When I sold my work at the flea market in Albuquerque, most of the people there found my work disturbing. I was told that I need psychiatric care, was asked if I had a bad childhood, and it was suggested to me on numerous occasions that maybe I should paint sunsets and landscapes.

I often tried to conform. Sometimes I would take a break from zombies and paint religious icons, trees, animals, and flowers. This would get the approval of some people but would leave me feeling detached from my own work. I would find myself frustrated by my lack of interest in the subjects of my own paintings and I'd guiltily go back to zombies. Eventually I realized that the ones who rejected my work didn't matter because they weren't in my target market anyway.

There's an axiom regarding public speaking which states that the instant one expresses an opinion, half the room already hates what your saying. Personally, I think it's more of a forty-forty split with twenty percent waiting to see which way the crowd goes. Once you understand that opinions will always be varied and that you cannot control the horde as it is, you'll see that there's no point trying to please too many people at once. The last time I sold art at the flea market, I was told by one shopper that my work was "Satanic." Instead of getting offended by the remark, I accepted it as feedback, telling me that I was clearly in the wrong place.

The Active Pursuit of Uniqueness vs Default Conformity

Until you're ready to take a stand, however, it is important to have a strategy for remaining under the radar and undetected among the undead. In zombie films, you'll notice that the survivors, the smart ones, will observe "light and sound discipline," a tactic used by ground troops in enemy territory in which they keep their lights dim and their voices low to avoid giving away their location.

Once you've openly declared war, there's no turning back. When you put your ideas out there, you have to stay in front of them. Competitors steal ideas the way zombies eat brains. Protect your brain and all of its contents. Your distinctive characteristics are what give your customers something to grasp on to, that firm foothold on what defines your brand. Being "definable" is critical for maximizing word of mouth advertising.

When people ask who you are or what your brand stands for, you need to be readily identifiable and memorable, in addition to searchable. Your brand must become synonymous with your niche, kind of like how people use the term "podcasting" even if they aren't referring to Ipods. The Ipod introduced its own lexicon, which in turn entered common usage among consumers. You rarely hear the word "microblogged", if at all, because companies like Twitter have dominated the discourse with their own lexicon.

To rise above the horde you'll have to abandon the false sense of security that conformity offers. That security comes at a price: it will cost you the potential rewards that result from intelligent risk taking. Another advantage to doing things your own way is that you'll love what you do. Doing what one loves and believes in results in a sense of pride, more passion, and greater satisfaction with the work.

There's no passion in conformity; only apathy, averageness, and predictability. While the potential for failure can never be omitted entirely, it can be mitigated by strategically turning your uniqueness into an advantage and having the confidence to be the "the nail that sticks out."

Chapter 16: Find Your Death Ground

A few years ago I violently disassembled my smartphone. It was a purely a business decision. It was a costly distraction and ceased to be compatible with my art-centric life. Many people were puzzled by my seemingly rash decision, after all, why would someone destroy a perfectly good phone instead of simply unplugging it? At that time in my life, it was truly getting in the way. Too many people were calling, texting, and interrupting my work, and worst of all, I was complicit in these distractions. So, I made the executive decision to go phoneless for a while.

In the Art of War, Sun Tzu prescribes the strategy of creating a "death ground" to motivate an army. It's intended to elicit the greatest effort by eliminating all escape routes. The rationale for this is based upon a solid understanding of human nature and the self-preservation instinct. In the face of insurmountable odds, soldiers with low morale might lose interest in battle and seek to avoid confrontation. Unmotivated, non incentivised soldiers may not put forth their best effort---a perfectly understandable response when faced with a high probability of death. So, in order to motivate the army, a wise general, according to this advice, should put them into "Death Ground".

Death Ground is what's left when all options are narrowed down to a single imperative: win or die. This is accomplished by burning all bridges, food rations, and eliminating the possibility of retreat. Without safety nets or contingency plans, a total focus upon the objective is the only option. The level of concentration attained in this manner overrides inhibition, lack of motivation, and inertia.

The key to achieving the focused concentration of the Death Ground is the elimination of alternative paths to a goal. It is human nature to seek out and choose the path of least resistance. In the absence of clear and present dangers, the stressors of competition, or the element of risk, stagnation invariably sets in.

Your workspace must become your Death Ground if you intend to make the most out of your time. This may require shutting off, if not destroying, your cellphone. Use music, white noise, or silence--whichever serves to cut you off from anything competing for your attention. Your Death

Ground is like a cocoon or an incubator. Its sanctity cannot be taken for granted.

A fortified dwelling amidst legions of the living dead can only enable your survival to the extent that your maintain its boundaries. One loose board, one missing nail, or one unbarricaded door is all it takes to admit an influx of murderous cannibal zombies. If you're not willing to jettison the myriad of entertaining distractions, then you're leaving failure on the table as an option. Find your Death Ground, board up your windows, barricade the doors, and focus on your brand's survival.

Phase 4:Surviving The Second Wave

Anything Goes in the Zombie Apocalypse

"A man who wants to act virtuously in every way necessarily comes to grief among so many who are not virtuous." Niccolo Machiavelli

The zombie apocalypse renders traditional ways of doing things futile. Old rules haven't been replaced, just made irrelevant. For those committed to the way things have always been, the changes result in obsolescence and extinction. To the adaptable and opportunistic entrepreneur, it is a chance to compete on equal grounds with larger, and better funded, established brands.

Smartphones and other portable devices have made interconnectivity the norm. Even people that were initially reluctant or unwilling to create their own social media accounts have been drawn into it. As with any revolutionary changes--and the breakdown of traditional media structures is a revolutionary, apocalyptic change--those who are quick to recognize the shifting tides will come out on top, while those are will not budge from their routines will find themselves overwhelmed when the inevitable changes arrive. Just ask your local newspaper how, or if, they're surviving.

Each emerging micro market has the potential to disrupt and take revenue from the mass market they can now compete with. The creators can focus on what they choose, not what they think will sell. The new interconnectivity means that no one is unreachable. Like a rapidly spreading plague of undeath, it's only a matter of time before your targeted customers reach you via your mutual involvement in your niche. When your brand has become synonymous with your niche, your sales will become almost automatic, and your role will evolve from actively seeking customers to passively fulfilling a demand.

Chapter 17: Eliminate the Muddle Man

"The forces of powerful ally can be useful and good to those who have recourse to them, but are perilous to those who become dependent on them."

--Niccolo Machiavelli, The Prince

Every mediator in a transaction will affect that which is mediated. In painting, when too many colors are mixed in, it eventually assumes a mud like color and consistency. In physics this is called Attenuation, or more appropriately for this context, Extinction. This refers to the gradual loss in intensity in any kind of flux through a medium.

Just as sunlight can be attenuated with sunglasses, so too will the success of your brand be attenuated by each *muddle* man you employ. Like divinely inspired texts in the hands of theocratic despots, your brand will be distorted to reflect the interests of the curator you work with.

Essentially, the relationship between the individual creator and the middle man is one of power. The mediator is a conduit who extracts a fee for facilitating access to an exclusive place, body of knowledge, or an exclusive gallery. Like a dragon in a secretary's seat, the mediator is in a position of control and power. Not because they deserve it, or even desire it, but because they have access to something you need. However much the middle man purports to be acting in your best interests, it's worth bearing in mind that no one can possibly care as much about your success as you do.

This is not meant to impugn those who hold these positions. It just means that their relevance is fading. Why would a musician hire an agent or sign a contract if directly selling music online means higher royalties? There are many valid reasons why you might want to cooperate with and work with those who have access, information, and expertise, however, it makes a lot of sense to also be capable of functioning independently.

I sell my art independently, but anytime an opportunity arises to work with a gallery or an event organizer, I am open to it. My point here is that one must eschew dependencies. Treat the middle man as a stepping stone, or an ally, but never as a gatekeeper:

The middle man, the curator, the agent, and the popular person with all the right connections have all lost their status as gatekeepers. They're going the way of the dinosaurs. Social media is the asteroid which fragmented the mass markets put the mass marketing dinosaurs on the path to Extinction. Your brand must evolve with the times if it is to survive under these new conditions.

Chapter 18: Release The Horde. Social Media Mobbing

Mobs on the Internet are not all that different from the kinds that gather in the streets. They can be creative and cunning, as well as destructive and brutish. They can go either way, it's just a matter of properly channeling the energy towards the desired aims.

Mobs can be generated for a specific purpose at a particular time, as can be seen every Black Friday, or they can be spontaneously executed as with flash mobs. Then there are "smart mobs", which are highly choreographed publicity stunts.

Mobs are effective because they are too big to ignore. They take over the public space and become the five-hundred pound gorilla in the room. Political mobs derive their strength from their visibility; the more attention they receive, the bigger they grow. Religious mobs can be large or small, most beginning as cults before metastasizing into megachurches with congregations numbering in the hundreds of thousands.

Like Dr. Frankenstein's Monster or an out of control android, a mob can lose respect for the will of its creator, or worse, it can take on the characteristics of its more extreme constituents. One constructive use for a mob is getting your social media followers to promote a particular product, meme, or event. The more you can engage them, the more support you can get. It's a simple matter of finding a motivator.

A negative use for a mob would be suggesting to your followers that they boycott a certain seller or promote your brand on the page of a competitor. Just never order a mob as though it were your personal army. If the cause is just, they merely have to be pointed in the right direction, and the mob will act on its own accord. Mobs tend to resent being treated like fodder. Allowing them the freedom to act on their own absolves you from the consequences of their actions.

When you're attempting to concentrate a large number of people into a cyber mob or a street mob, the most critical part is getting all the participants on the same schedule. Mobbing is all about timing. The more participants within a specified time frame the greater their effect will be.

If you're releasing something new, like a book or an album, the way to build a mob on the release date is to put out a teaser or a sample. It must contain a call to action which prompts the potential buyer to subscribe for updates or to download an app which will enable them to receive a notification on the date of release. Taking pre-orders is one way to make this happen.

Mobs can be incentivised with discounts in exchange for product reviews or by offering rewards for sharing the event on their social media pages. Each event will require a hashtag, a Facebook Page, and a press release.

Given the sheer volume of competing voices on the Internet, there is an inherent difficulty in monopolizing an audience's attention, even for a few seconds. The "buzz worthiness" of your product has to be measured against the competition. For this reason, you'll have to coordinate your mobs to either avoid pre existing events or to merge with them. For instance, release a new product on Black Friday or Cyber Monday since you know that the shoppers are out en masse and are prepared to spend.

Merging with preexisting events is a practical alternative to ginning up your own crowds. For example, find conventions or trade shows where your product will find a receptive audience. If you find an event which caters to your own targeted markets, find out all you can about it in advance. Go to its social media pages and look at the invitations to see who plans to attend. Since I sell Zombie Art, I can sell my work at any number of zombie themed events, such as "zombie crawls" or horror movie conventions.

A comment about employing agitators:

People today are weary of spam. They are not receptive to ham fisted advertising attempts. Therefore, it's better to try and merge with pre existing mobs or to organically grow your own, than to try to force one into existence. However, should you need to stir up a social media mob on short notice, you can use "zombie accounts", also known as "sock puppet" accounts on any social media site and directly promote your website or products by following, subscribing, friending, or tagging people who fall into your target demographic. In order to avoid being detected, you'll want to have a stable of such accounts ready to be deployed on short notice. Just build them up over time, or better yet, outsource the maintenance of your "zombie account" stable so that when they are unleashed, they don't appear to be shills.

Chapter 19: Turf Wars in the Zombie Apocalypse

It's not just zombies that want a piece of your brain. A greater threat often comes from among the living. Some people choose to take from others rather than generate their own ideas. While it can be vexing or even flattering in some ways, you must take into account that in a Post-Apocalyptic world, resources are scarce.

The niche or micro market places your brand into a relatively small pond, and as the expression goes, "small pond, many big fish." What this means is that you must be vigilant about who you are sharing your pond with. Friendly competition is a good thing since the more individuals that contribute to the niche, the more you all benefit. After all, you're all in cooperation against the undead, right? Sadly, that's not true all of the time.

Sharing a niche can be productive to a certain degree, however, there are times when the competition ceases to be friendly. For example, unscrupulous competitors can sabotage your hard work with negative reviews. Or your ideas might be misappropriated. Thankfully, when you're in the right, it's not difficult to turn the followers of a copycat into your own followers.

In my experience, the term "copycat" is something of a misnomer; it doesn't even begin to properly describe the true character of the intellectual property thief. From the seemingly harmless mimic to the vainglorious poseur, there are many shades of unoriginal-rat-bastard, but what they all have in common is that they are easy to deal with as long as you're aware of their tactics and intrinsic weaknesses.

Think of a copycat as a low-grade stalker. They may not want to rifle through your personal belongings but what they do want is far more insidious: a piece of your soul. The copycat feels nothing about taking from you. The way to handle such a person is simple: stalk them back. Locate all of their social media accounts and websites. Then, make your case on a blog post by showing how your ideas were stolen.

If you can make the case, then all you have to do is gin up a little cyber lynch mob. This requires little more than messaging a few agitators, those who are loyal to your brand, with a link to the blog post. The blog post should contain a call to action, perhaps asking readers to post a link to the blog on your target's social media accounts. This confrontation is not between you and your copycat, but rather between your copycat, and both yours and his followers. Cyber Mobs are very intimidating and can ruin a reputation in moments. After you have incited one, you can contact your copycat directly and demand a public apology. Your words will have more gravitas when an angry mob is standing at your back.

Another way to deal with unfriendly competition is to play dirty. One tactic is to create "zombie accounts" to create mayhem on their social media, to ruin their ratings with negative reviews, and to buy out their for sale merchandise with no intention of paying for any of it. These tactics will disrupt their operation and temporarily cut off their sales.

Unscrupulous tactics have their place, especially in the anything goes atmosphere of a zombie apocalypse. Imagine how you would react if your fortified house was being raided by a neighbor. Imagine you're both fighting the hordes off and your neighbor has the audacity to steal your building supplies to block his own windows. Would you not be justified in tearing his door off and using it to make your home more secure? It's not as if you're burning his house down. You're just letting a few zombies in, that's all. I would contend that you're justified in doing unto others as they have done unto you, so long as you don't get the blood (or brains) on your own hands.

Chapter 20: No Such Thing as Bad Publicity

No news may be good news in most contexts, but for the purposes of building a brand, the absence of feedback is bad news. Feedback comes in many forms, not just reviews. Every time a person comments, subscribes, or otherwise interacts with your products through your websites and social media, they are providing you valuable feedback. Their decision to click their mouse implies that you were noticed, and attention is the currency of brand awareness. If you're holding attention, then you're accumulating capital.

There's an axiom about how a good customer service experience will be heard be shared with one or two people, but a negative one will be emphatically shared with anyone who will listen. When I worked at a pizza restaurant as a teenager, this made perfect sense. A stray pepperoni on an otherwise vegetarian pizza would cause each herbivore partaking of it to choose a different restaurant the next time. A properly made pizza consistent with the order, however, is too normal and expected an occurrence to warrant any further discussion. People generally don't become emotionally wound up over routine, problem free experiences, but disrupt their expectations with bad service and your brand will never live it down, even if a refund is provided in a timely manner.

It is important not to interpret bad reviews as anything other than signifiers that your brand has made an unforgettable impact. The trick to making the most out of a bad review is to address it in a way that shows your human side. It's only human to act offended, indignant, and defensive. If you truly don't deserve it, then give the bad review a bad review, publicly. Tweet it to your followers. Make a joke about it. Lambast your detractors and your followers will too. If you do deserve it, make your apology and restitution public to show that you are trustworthy and honorable.

Pithy rebuttals to undeservedly critical reviews are especially well suited to social media and can elicit the support of your followers in the form of comments, "shares," and "Retweets". Treat bad reviews as opportunities to strengthen your brand. This will more than compensate you for the hassle of rectifying a complaint.

Good reviews are better than self-promotion which is why testimonials have been used to promulgate products, ideas, services, religious faiths, and brands long before the advent of the public relations industry and mass marketing. Good reviews are granted a degree of credibility according to the source of the testimonial. Anonymous reviews are always suspect and self-promotion is assumed to be biased, but when others do the evangelizing for you, it rings truer.

Here are two reviews, the first of which isn't necessarily complementary, yet it is the most widely read review of my artwork. The first is a "bad" review, and the second is a "good" review. Both of them, however, are marketing gold:

1) Review of Jack Larson's art at www.Cracked.com:

".....If you own an Android phone or tablet, you know that it's good to update it every once in awhile because each new version comes with nifty new features and ways to accidentally message photos of your genitals to everyone in your family. What you might not know is that each version also comes with a cool Easter egg -- like this adorable painting of the Android mascot standing next to a monstrous gingerbread man and surrounded by a bunch of zombies talking on phones via Android

"We'd be offended by the implication, but we're too busy being creeped out. Yes, that's in your phone, and yes, it looks like something Jeffrey Dahmer painted in first grade. In order to see the Easter egg, simply go to your Settings menu and tap "About Phone." You'll see "Android Version" in that menu. Tap on that part very fast a bunch of times, and eventually a reward will pop onto your screen..."

2) Review of Jack Larson's art in the Albuquerque Alibi

"Bloody zombies in tuxedos at a wedding of the damned, a ghoul who looks kind of like Pinhead from Hellraiser, Roswell aliens and dead-eyed pooches—these are just some of the ingredients that make up Jack Larson's disarmingly crude paintings. And the result is a maniacally eerie world that meets somewhere between the minds of George Romero and Edvard Munch.

The artist sums up his work with one brief Romero quote: "When there's no more room in hell, the dead will walk the earth ... ." A theme to notice: Larson's undead are all coming to get us—their arms outstretched, attempting to break free of the canvas and shred human flesh."

Phase 5: Post-Pandemic: From Surviving to Thriving

"Keep walking." --- Rick, The Walking Dead

There is always more work to be done, even when you've established your brand. The more successful you become the easier it will be to automate much of the work. Spreading a virus is a lot like setting a fire. Every once in awhile you'll have to add more fuel to the fire but as long as you don't allow it to go out, it doesn't require a whole lot of maintenance. Post-Pandemic is the maintenance phase. This is when you monitor the spread of the virus and adjust your efforts accordingly.

When you have a Strain or a formula that works you no longer have to revise and reinvent. Instead, you can focus on growing the horde. As long as remain focused on taking consistent actions, your virus will spread. The strategy employed at this stage is to move towards automation. Zombies are natural automatons and to a great extent are programmable. You can accomplish more with fewer resources and using less time by removing yourself as much as possible from the equation.

The more autonomous your marketing campaign becomes, the more you can make the transition from surviving to thriving. For example, I have turned many of my designs into products, such as coffee mugs and tshirts, and these are produced by a third party that takes care of order fulfillment on my behalf. When I receive royalty payments, I turn around and reinvest it into advertisements aimed at enlarging my Facebook following.

Surviving by scavenging or hunting is time consuming and risky. Thriving can only happen when you've liberated yourself from immersion in tasks which can be delegated and automated. It's important to plan for Phase 5. You might have a solid business or product, let's say for example, the best hotdog stand in town. Regardless of how good those hot dogs happen to be, if you're personally responsible for each and every hotdog, you'll always live or die by the work of your own two hands. It's only when you open multiple stands and hire staff that you can focus on thriving.

The key concept at this phase is scalability. Make what you do scalable. Make your virus metastasize. For me, I am adding new products to my store each day, one by one. Eventually, I'll have a sizable catalog of products incorporating my designs. This creates value for me in several ways. Most notably, it extends the life of each painting as both a marketing tool and a source of revenue. Instead of surviving painting to painting, I am working towards automating my entire operation so that whether I am painting or not, I am still earning and my business is still growing.

The following chapters deal with growth, scalability, and automation.

Chapter 21: Breaking Dirt Ceilings

I have a term for people who use fear as an excuse to avoid change. I call them "moldy people." Moldy people remain so committed to their molds, to stagnation, that they acquire moldy, fungal growths, and begin to decay prematurely.

The moldiest ones can often be observed projecting their fears onto others, attempting to confine others to their own molds. There is nothing positive or helpful in trying to keep others within their comfort zones. Naysayers, who tend to be very moldy, are known for their good intentions. The fact is, failure can be scary and some people succumb to that fear.

It is important to know when you're dealing with molds that have been imposed upon your thinking. Most limitations are self-imposed. Negative self-talk tends to manifest in self-fulfilling prophecy. Do you have a fear of public speaking? Or is it just that you've always heard it said that public speaking is scary? If you have never tried, then you've been in a mold. A mold in which you are not a public speaker.

Moldy people are prisoners to the fear of failure. It is not humanly possible to be right all of the time and even if it was, failure often happens because of the unpredictable and the unexpected. But like it or not, failure is a necessary part of refinement. Consider the number of iterations communication technologies have gone through since the telegraph. We don't look back at rotary phones and deride them as failures. We know that those were cutting edge at the time.

Instead of personalizing failures, consider them within the context of experimentation. Experimentation is a necessary part of growth. Whatever your particular product or service happens to be, if your operation is prematurely scaled up in size, then the problem areas which could have been detected by experimentation will also increase in size. Small problems don't go away when they are subsidized or enabled. They just become big problems.

Here is an example. I sold my art through online auctions and did all of the order fulfillment myself. On several occasions, the demand for my work made it possible for me to sell more art than I actually had the time to package and ship. Consequently, my customer service suffered and I ended up losing money rather than benefiting from increased sales. By rigidly conforming to my business model as a one man operation, I hit a ceiling when it came to my productive capacity.

I was forced to rethink my approach and in the process I exposed several problems. For one thing, I was spending way too much time at the post office. The inefficiencies were costing me time that could have been invested into research and development. When I finally was forced to take some time off because of a failure to pay my auction fees on time, I experimented with hiring an assistant and I looked into third party shipping companies.

Eventually, I settled on printing my own shipping labels from home and arranged for the postman to pick up the art from my front porch. Then I hired someone to list my auction items for me. By making these minor adjustments, I liberated two to three hours a day, or about twenty hours per week. In those twenty or so hours, I was able to produce more and thus, I was able to pay my employee with what I earned in those hours I salvaged.

In the earlier phases of this strategy, you'll be finding what works and standardizing it. However, as your zombie virus progresses and promulgates itself into your target market, your focus will have to adjust. You must look up and prepare to punch or claw your way out of the coffin, through six feet of dirt, and work your way up to the surface. You may ingest the occasional worm here and there, but as long as you're moving upward, it will be worth it.

Nobody can break your mold for you. Nobody is going to dig you up. It is up to you to dig your way up and then to drag others to the surface. You will need others that you can delegate responsibilities to. In my example above, I delegated shipping duties to the postman instead of carrying the packages myself and waiting in line. I delegated the auction listings to someone I trained myself.

You will know your business is scalable when you've made it possible for it to continue without you having to micromanage every aspect of it. Break your business model down into a disparate set of interconnected tasks. Take your hourly rate and calculate how much the money you save by outsourcing. Micromanagement is what you do in the beginning phases of building your brand. That's the part where you develop your zombie virus and test it out. That's when you experiment and learn from the failures and successes on a micro scale. World Zombification can only happen when you're free to focus on the big picture, on Macromanagment.

Chapter 22: Sustainable Mindless Consumption

Your horde wants to grow. All it needs is access to the living. As a Macromanager seeking to increase the size of your horde, you must ensure that it keeps moving. Never allow your horde to be corralled or cut off from the where the living congregate. Locate the quarantined zones and infiltrate your Zombie Virus by employing whatever methods are at your disposal.

Dead links are to new customers what blocked freeways or burned bridges are to a ravenous pack of zombies. Accessibility is everything. If you're not active on your social media page, at least be sure that the posts that newcomers see have hot links that are active.

The only thing predictable about marketing tactics is that the results are usually unpredictable. While you can count on certain results to accompany specific efforts, you can't predict when something will go viral. "Forced memes" are memes that are aggressively pushed with the expectation that forced exposure will result in a viral marketing success. Forced memes don't really work any more than regular advertising efforts which rely on repetition. Forcing memes into the mass consciousness is a mass marketing tactic, and not a very sustainable one at that.

Many guerilla marketing tactics are passive, like booby-traps. What makes such tactics part of a sustainable strategy is the fact that you don't have to invest into passive marketing tactics once they have been put into place. There is nothing sustainable about standing on a street corner and trying to share your opinions by shouting at passing cars. What will get your opinions heard is the strategic placement of your words, whether you write them on a blog or state them on video. A blog or a video will always be there to attract relevant readers and viewers. Once it is published, there is no more upkeep required.

In my own business, I have moved away from selling individual paintings and shifted my focus into selling prints and related products generated with my designs from several third party companies who also handle order fulfillment. Even if I were to slip into a coma today, my work would still be out there selling in one form or another and I would be receiving royalties. If I were to remain a one man operation, a period of sickness could ruin my entire business.

Your horde's ability to sustain itself as it mindlessly consumes its way across the planet is dependent upon your ability to Macromanage. When you've successfully become a Macromanager, the operation will continue to thrive, even if its head is cut off.

Chapter 23: Force Multipliers. 23 Ways to Grow a Zombie Horde

The purpose of growing your horde is to enable you to achieve maximum results with the least amount of micromanaging. You can't be a general and a foot soldier simultaneously. To exponentially increase the size and scope of your operation you must become a Macromanager. To become a Macromanager, you'll need a HIT Team, an Intelligence Network, and a Virtual Staff.

The following suggestions should be tailored to your specific needs. If you can employ all twenty-three of them, you'll be well on your way to achieving World Zombification:

1) Always Leave a Mark

Post a link to your website in your email signature. This can be done in the settings portion of your email provider. If you have a mobile phone app, embed it there as well. This simple act will turn your every email into a marketing tool. Also, turn on your "vacation responder" so that when you're unable to respond to emails in a timely manner, your prospects will still be greeted with an informative message with relevant links.

2) Take Names

Build your email list by posting advertisements for the kinds of things your buyers would be interested in. For instance, if you find your niche with sports, then you could post an advertisement for a soccer equipment on free classified ads. Give your email address out in the ad. Then, when someone emails you about it, you can reply with "yes, I still have it," or "no, sorry, sold it already." Whether or not you actually buy the equipment and resell it is immaterial. People who like soccer and need soccer equipment will be emailing you. Each person you respond to will see website url and mobile app unobtrusively displayed under the body of your email, and more importantly, they will inadvertently add themselves to your list.

3) Employ Dynamic Web Content

Embed Twitter, Instagram, and Pinterest widgets on all your blogs and websites so even if you abandon a blog or move on to another project, the customer will still see your current content and contact information.

4) Use Proxies to Infiltrate Social Media Networks

I sometimes offer free art in exchange for a customer making it their profile picture. Getting others to advertise on your behalf effectively advertises to their followers. Word of mouth referrals are easy to obtain if you find ways to incentivise others to evangelize your brand for you.

5) Propaganda Blitz

Create multiple blogs and have them all setup for posting by email. This will make it possible to update several blogs by sending a single email. be sure that email has your website and mobile app in the signature area. The blogs don't have to relate to your product or brand directly. For instance, if you review books or music, or perhaps you just write social commentary, you might still attract the right customers. Maintaining a blog is an important part of your overall marketing strategy because it adds to your searchability and it functions as a catalog. Each blog post generates a unique URL so stick with a consistent set of relevant keywords. Provide links to all your social network accounts with every post. Since you'll be posting by email, make sure you have a good email signature (see #1).

6) Invest in Free Samples

Don't be afraid to give free samples away. Most people are happy to receive free gifts and many will happily show their support by keeping a small stack of your business cards. If you're giving away digital products, then do so in exchange for a social media plug.

7) Self-Produce Your Marketing Materials

Create your own business cards, brochures, and flyers with any digital photo editing software at 300 dpi. Email your image to a local photo lab and order prints. Printing your own cards means you can have several dozen of these prints prepared for just a few dollars, usually in under an hour, and you'll never be stuck paying too much for several thousand identical cards. There are many websites that offer high quality, free templates. I recommend Lucidpress.com and Canva.com.

8) Start an Email Newsletter

Create an email newsletter for building long-term relationships through periodic contact. Incentivise followers by offering coupon codes for new subscribers and other special offers for existing subscribers.

9) Access Target Markets with Free Classifieds

Use free sites like Craigslist.com to advertise because they tend to show up very well in search engines. Don't restrict yourself to posting in the appropriate categories. For example, if you're marketing a book, instead of posting it in the "books" section, post it where the relevant potential customers will be searching. So if your book is about how to build a backyard water fountain, then post it in the section where landscapers are searching for gigs. When landscapers see your post, they might be inclined to consider adding fountains as part of their landscaping business. Posting advertisements is a menial task and so it would behoove you to write your advertisement copy and then outsource the posting duties (see #16 for how to outsource menial tasks inexpensively).

10) Wait Marketing

Have a sample chapter or short story printed as pamphlet. Place it in places where the people who encounter it will have a use for it, such as at the DMV or your local laundromats where reading material can alleviate boredom. Follow the marketing tactics of the Watchtower Society and other organizations that take advantage of places where people expect to be bored.

If you're selling artwork, you could have it printed into pamphlets. If your product or service isn't literary or artistic, such as website design, you can still place your materials in such locations however you'll have to give the potential buyer something to interact with for this tactic to work.

Here are a couple examples of this tactic:

a. I picked up a free poster advertising a comic book. I was in a restaurant awaiting my order and realized that the poster was designed to be folded into an airplane. The airplane was printed with a winged character from the comic book, so the paper plane was actually a flying superhero. It was a clever idea because it caused me to engage with it without realizing I was being advertised to.

b. If you are a clothing designer, you could cheaply produce brochures featuring your clothing line, and slip them into magazines in waiting rooms. Just be sure to use QR codes or urls in order to direct the prospect to your online store.

11) Target Mobile Devices

Mobile Apps are the new business card: use mobile phone apps to promote your business. Whatever your field, you can find some kind of mobile app which will be relevant to the needs or desire of your target market. For instance, if you're a professional pet groomer, then you could have your website converted into a mobile app, for free in most cases, and offer weekly coupon codes which are only accessible through the app. Apps also allow customers to receive push button notifications to remind them to schedule an appointment. Just search for "Website to App" and you'll find a many websites that will convert your website into a mobile application..

12) A Picture is Worth 1000 Word of Mouth Advertisements

Use image sites such as Flickr to post your advertisements and share pictures of your product or service. There's a lot of people browsing Flickr every day, and it has a great search function built right in. Sign up for a free account, put up some content, properly tagged, of course,and place links to your website in the captions.

Take advantage of all the free image site because they will bring you traffic that you otherwise may have missed. I also recommend Tumblr, Twitter, and Imageshack. I have an application that allows me to post to several image websites simultaneously. Include a call to action, for example, "Share this image and get free shipping on your next order".

13) Get in Front of the Camera

Create video content introducing your products or services. Video blogs are great for drawing targeted traffic. The video doesn't have to be directly related to your product. For example, if you sell stereo equipment, you could acquire public domain music and upload it to Youtube and in the video description, post a link to purchase new speakers or headphones. You can even add captions to the videos in progress suggesting that the listener invest in better speakers to fully appreciate the music. Voice actors can be employed to read your content for you, thus sparing you the time and effort that goes into quality video and sound production. Never be afraid to outsource.

14) Solicit the Opinions of Popular People

This is not the same as shilling, where you pay people to pretend to like your product. Paid reviewers are more like test-audiences, but instead of keeping their feedback private and using it to guide your decisions, you instead pay them to react to your product naturally and share their response. For example, send a free sample to someone on facebook in exchange for them posting about it on their own timeline. Or, you could ask someone with a video blog to mention your product during a video, and pay them an affiliate fee or a commission on sales.

15) Guerilla Marketing

Place promotional material in related books at a major chain bookstore. For example, if you teach self-defense,put your business card in the self-defense books. You can also get away with this at the public library. I like to purchase horror novels about zombies and after I read them I sell them on Ebay, including a bookmark printed with my own artwork.

16) Build a HIT Team

Integrate Amazon.com HITs into your marketing strategy. HITs, or "Human Intelligence Tasks", is a labor pool you can access through Amazon. This is where you can post minor tasks which will be handled by qualified workers who do HITs on a part or full time basis.

Here's an example: you could post a task requiring someone to set up an email account and use it to create blog, a Twitter account, a Facebook account, and a Youtube account. Such a task would cost a couple of dollars if not less. Then you would post another task which would include adding content to each of the social media accounts that were opened. You would provide the content.

This is how it would come together: for ten dollars, you could have your video advertisements posted to a new Youtube account, shared on a new Twitter account, and then posted on a Facebook page and blog. HITs will save you time and enable you to do more work than you could do on your own. Future tasks could include updating all the accounts and growing these social networks.

17) Create Promotional Items

"Print on demand" websites such as Society6.com and Zazzle.com allow users to upload their own graphics and have them made available on shirts, stickers, keychains, coffee mugs, and more. Such websites handle all of the order fulfillment and then pay you a royalty. However, the purpose isn't to sell your items. While that may happen, the real benefit to listing them is to allow them to serve as advertisements. Free advertisements.

The listings you create can be shared on your social media accounts and they will also get traffic from the website's own advertising efforts. Additionally, as a creator, you'll get discounts when you place orders of your own. This is a good way to acquire promotional materials, to advertise online, and to earn royalties.

If you're not inclined to format your own images and designs, you could find out the image requirements for each item and then outsource the tasks of formatting and listing to your HIT team. As an artist, I never run out of materials to convert into promotional items. If you're not in the art business, you can hire a graphic designer to produce some designs for you. Many have their own stock images or you could find your own at a number of websites such as istockphoto.com or imageshack.us.

18) Make Waves (Get on the Radio)

The Internet has facilitated the emergence of talk shows on a variety of platforms, such as BlogTalkRadio.com, Youtube, and some are conducted over Skype. Find a few shows where you can appear as a guest to talk about what it is that you do, or start your own if you're so inclined. The technical side of it is hardly complicated.

If you're not inclined to do talk show formats then create an advertisement and approach talkshows that attract the kind of audience you want to reach. All you have to do is write the ad copy. Voice actors are everywhere and for a thirty second advertisement you won't have to pay more than twenty to fifty dollars. I posted a couple ads for voice actors just to see what kind of talent was out there, and I was inundated with attractive offers, some even offering to do work for free just to build their portfolios.

19) Hire a Virtual Staff

Get a Rolodex or find a free Rolodex application for your mobile device. Use it to keep track of all the talented or useful individuals or businesses who may be of use to you or have been helpful in the past. A Rolodex, for those who may not know, is a device used for organizing personal contacts.

The app version is the same thing except it organizes business cards that you manually scan or photograph. The purpose is to have a virtual staff of qualified independent contractors on hand for various projects and tasks, for example, graphic designers, artists, voice actors, writers, and website designer.

20) Build an Intelligence Network

Use Google Alerts. These are email notifications which inform you whenever certain keywords or topics show up on the web. You'll want to monitor your name, your company name, your product name, and all associated hashtags that relate to your business.

This will keep you up to date on marketing opportunities. For example, anytime there is a "zombie crawl", anywhere in the world, I get a news alert. This allows me to comment, share, or otherwise interact with the website, blog, or news article. These are great for monitoring for trends, upcoming movies, or other events which you might otherwise have missed. This also allows you to monitor the web for comments or reviews related to your brand, positive or negative.

21) Open Door Policy

Accessibility is a two way street. Just as you reach into the marketplace and connect with your customers, your customers must be able to reach your customer service or technical support, and get a decent response back. Displeased customers will always be heard. It's only a question of who they will tell. Will they lodge their complaint with you or will with fifty of their friends?

Many surveys have shown that people are twice as likely to share a negative customer service experience than a positive one. One way you can mitigate that tendency is to handle complaints in as personal manner as feasible. You could set up a dedicated voicemail for complaints, concerns, and even positive feedback. With Skype or Google Phone, you can arrange to have those voicemails delivered to your email as transcribed audio files. You can even mask your personal number through your Internet phone service provider, and make personal contact without compromising your privacy. People are more likely to rage against a faceless, impersonal entity than an actual human being.

Another benefit to this level of openness is that you'll leave yourself open to being contacted by those who can really help you. For example, there is a conspiracy theorist on Youtube who became popular for positing the notion that the Earth is the center of the universe. He gave his real name and real phone number in every quirky video, and eventually, a scout for a national radio talk show gave him a call and he scored a guest appearance on a show with millions of listeners. In other words, don't make them beat the door down to get to you. Invite them in.

22) Collaborate

The more people who have a vested interest in the success of an operation the better. Compare the following two strategies:

    a. A self-representing poet publishes a book of poetry and markets it to his or her own social network.

b. Ten poets get together and publish a collection of poetry in a single volume. Each of the them get their own chapter.

The difference is obvious. The ten poets invested into a single publication would bring ten different social media networks, ten sets of families, and ten sets of personal friends into the marketing equation.

23) DO WHAT <u>YOU</u> LOVE

About the Author

(Zombie Portrait by Rick Ormortis Schreck)

Jack Larson is an artist based out of Albuquerque, New Mexico. His work is mostly displayed in private collections around the world. Several of his paintings have been published as book covers and one has been featured as an "Easter Egg" within Android smartphones. His work has been excoriated in reviews, exorcised by fundamentalist preachers, and appreciated by art collectors since he started painting in 2009.

Find out more about Jack at his website
www.ZombieArt.blogspot.com
or follow him on:
Instagram @zombiemarketing
Twitter www.twitter.com/zombieart
Facebook www.Facebook.com/ZombieArtist

The Art of Jack Larson

www.ingramcontent.com/pod-product-compliance
Lightning Source LLC
Chambersburg PA
CBHW072306200526
45168CB00014B/873